ENGLISCHTIGER

Bestell-Nr. 1902-72 ISBN 978-3-619-19272-4

www.mildenberger-verlag.de
E-Mail: info@mildenberger-verlag.de

Auflage 4 3 2 1

Jahr 2020 2019 2018 2017

Entwickelt unter Nutzung von: Rabbit 1 – 6 My English Workbook, Mari Jonsson and Natur & Kultur, Stockholm
Überarbeitung: Friederike Beck, Witten

Redaktion: Axel Wolber
Grafik: Mildenberger Verlag GmbH
Illustrationen: Benjamin König, 85617 Lorenzenberg

Druck: Salzland Druck GmbH & Co. KG, 39418 Staßfurt

Contents

1 Write in the spaces.*

My name is ____________________

I am ____________________

I live in ____________________

2 Draw yourself or take a photo.

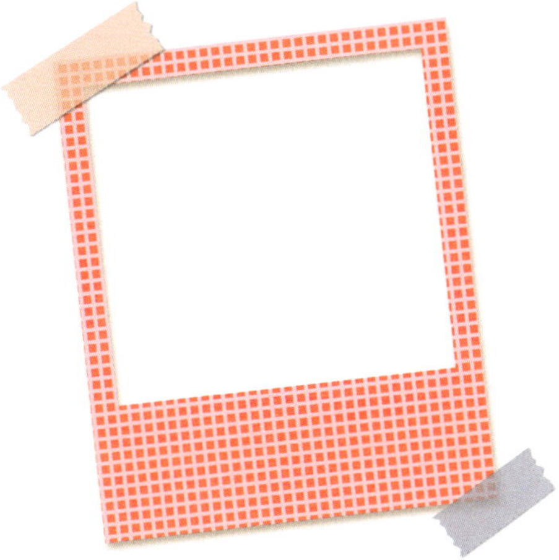

3 Enter a ☒ cross.*

☐ I'm a girl. ☐ I'm a boy.

I come from ☐ Germany.

I come from ☐ Turkey.

I come from ☐ Poland.

I come from ☐ Italy.

I come from ☐ Greece.

I come from ☐ ____________________

* Individuelle Lösungen

1 Unscramble and write.

r h e a t f | e h t r m o | r o b h t e r | s i r t e s

father ______ ______ ______

2 Draw your family or take a photo.

3 Enter a ✗ cross.

Do you have a sister?	☐ Yes	☐ No
Do you have a brother?	☐ Yes	☐ No
Do you have an aunt?	☐ Yes	☐ No
Do you have an uncle?	☐ Yes	☐ No
Do you have a grandma?	☐ Yes	☐ No
Do you have a grandpa?	☐ Yes	☐ No

I have ☐ ______

Have a look!

1  Fill in:

stars orange stripes guitar blue

2 Fill in:

blonde brown present orange green

New jeans

1 Fill in:

When	How	Why	Which	John	Louise

1 How many pairs of blue jeans do you have, John?

2 I have four pairs of blue jeans!

3 ________ do you want another pair of blue jeans?

4 Because I love blue jeans, Louise!

5 ________ other colours do you have, John?

6 I have green, red, brown, orange, yellow and black jeans.

7 ________ are you going to wear all these jeans?

8 I wear a different coloured pair of jeans every day, ________!

9 Oh ________, you are just like a girl!

2 Read the dialogue with a partner.

My hobbies

 What do you like to do? Write and  mark your answer with a  cross.

riding a bike | playing computer games | reading a book | swimming in the pool

singing a song | dancing to the music | cooking a meal | ~~writing a story~~

writing a

story

1 Unscramble, match and write.

__________ __________ sister __________ __________

2 Fill in the spaces and mark your answer with a ☒ cross.

Which | When | Where | How

__________ many books do you have? ☐ No books. ☐ More than five. ☐ More than ten.

__________ kinds of books do you like? ☐ Comics. ☐ Novels. ☐ Thrillers.

__________ do you read books? ☐ In my bed. ☐ Under a tree. ☐ In the living room.

__________ do you read books? ☐ After school. ☐ Before breakfast. ☐ During holidays.

In the morning

1 What time do you wake up in the morning?

Draw the time and write.

I wake up at ______________________

____

2 What time do you leave for school?

Draw the time and write.

____

____

____

3 How do you get to school?

Put a [X] in the right box.

I walk alone.	☐
I walk with a friend.	☐
I ride a bike.	☐
I go by car.	☐
I ride a scooter.	☐
I go by bus.	☐
I run because I'm always late.	☐

Breakfast time

1 Read and draw a line to the correct picture.

Write and complete all your sentences with these words:

bacon and eggs	
cat	~~glass of milk~~
dog	hair

You can drink a ... You can eat

You can eat ...

You can comb your ... You can drink a glass of milk

You can feed your ...

You can go for a walk with your ...

2 Read your sentences with a partner.

Your school

Write the answers.

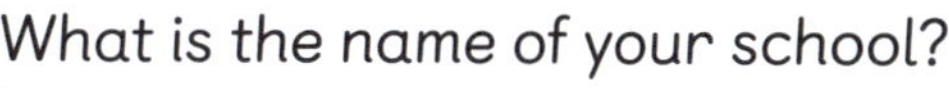

What is the name of your school?

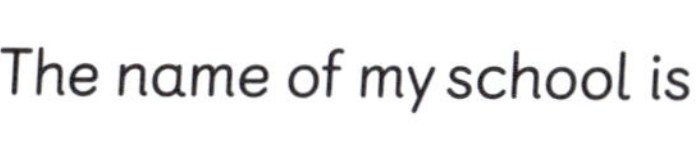

The name of my school is

______________________________.

Is it a big or a small school?

It's ______________________________.

How many children are there in your class?

______________________________.

How many girls are there in your class?

______________________________.

And how many boys?

______________________________.

What is your teacher's name?

______________________________.

What do you like to do at school? Put a ☒ in the box if you like doing it.

 What do you like best?

 I like ______________________________ best.

 What are you good at?

 I am good at ______________________________.

 In which subject would you like to get better at?

 I would like to get better at ______________________________.

The days of the week

1 Write in the spaces.

Please write them here.

Monday	Monday
Tuesday	
Wednesday	
Thursday	
Friday	
Saturday	
Sunday	

2 Write in the spaces.

What day is it today? ____________________

What day is it tomorrow? ____________________

Which is the best day of the week? ____________________

Why? ____________________

What can Indira and Alex do this week? Write in the spaces.

~~ride a bike~~	watch a movie	play football	ride a horse
tidy your room	play badminton	go for a picnic	

On Monday we can ride a bike. ______________________________

On Tuesday ______________________________ ______________________________

On ______________________________ ______________________________

______________________________ ______________________________

______________________________ ______________________________

______________________________ ______________________________

What do they love doing?

 Complete the sentences to the pictures:

... loves dancing.	... loves fishing.	loves playing football.	... loves swimming.

Mary

Luke

Lara

Alex

What do you love doing?

What does your best friend love doing?

How well do you know your best friend?

1 Think for a little while and enter a ☒ cross.

2 ☒ And now your friend!

Does he/she	Yes	No	Yes	No
play cards? 	☐	☐	☐	☐
play chess? 	☐	☐	☐	☐
play football? 	☐	☐	☐	☐
make biscuits? 	☐	☐	☐	☐
write letters? 	☐	☐	☐	☐
____________	☐	☐	☐	☐

3 Compare your answers with those of your friend.

How many same answers do you have? ______________________________

Would you like to ...

 What would you like to do?

Yes, I would. | No, I wouldn't.

Would you like to go up in a balloon? ____________________

Would you like to sky dive? ____________________

Would you like to be a successful author? ____________________

Would you like to swim with dolphins? ____________________

Would you like to be a famous musician? ____________________

That's what I know 1

1 Write the days of the week in the correct order.

Sunday ______________

Saturday ______________

Thursday ______________

Wednesday ______________

Friday ______________

Tuesday ______________

Monday ______________

2 Match.

write letters

play cards

play football

make biscuits

play chess

read books

play computer games

Parts of a house

1 Write the words for the parts of the house:

balcony roof door window spout bell

Itsy bitsy spider

D A D
1. The it-sy bit-sy spi-der climbed up the wa-ter-spout.

A7 D
Down came the rain and washed the spi - der out.

A D
Out came the sun and dried up all the rain and the

A7 D
it - sy bit-sy spi-der climbed up the spout a - gain._

2 Read and sing the nursery rhyme. How would you mime the words?

3 Colour the picture if you would like to.

Furniture

1 Match and write.

a bed	☐	a bedside table
a desk and a chair	☐	
a bedside table	☐	
a carpet	☐	
a wardrobe	☐	
a pinboard	☐	
a bookcase	☐	

2 Which furniture do you like? Put crosses in the boxes.

 Answer the questions.

CDs	lamp	blanket	carpet
books	cushion	~~painting~~	

What is hanging on the wall?

A painting .

Which things are lying on the sofa?

______________________________________.

Which things are standing on the narrow storage rack?

______________________________________.

What is lying under the sofa and the coffee table?

______________________________________.

Which things are standing on the shelf?

______________________________________.

What is standing behind the sofa?

______________________________________.

Where are the things?

1 Read and complete the sentences:

in near next to under on at the sides of

The television is __________ the brown cupboard.

The green carpet is ____________ the brown table.

The red lamp is _______________ the blue sofa.

The blue flower is _____________ the white vase.

The green houseplant is ______________ the brown cupboard.

The yellow curtains are _________________________ the window.

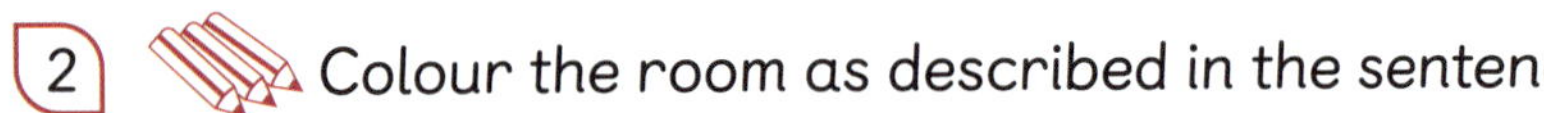

2 Colour the room as described in the sentences.

1 Count the things in the kitchen.

① ~~pot – pots~~	② cutting board – cutting boards	③ bowl – bowls	④ glass - glasses

⑤ flowerpot – flowerpots	⑥ coffee machine – coffee machines

one	one	three	eight	ten	~~twelve~~

① There are twelve pots.

② There is ______________________.

③ ______________________.

④ ______________________.

⑤ ______________________.

⑥ ______________________.

1 Write the numbers in the circles.

① ~~bathtub~~	② shower	③ washbasin	④ toothbrush	⑤ toothpaste	⑥ soap
⑦ hairbrush	⑧ comb	⑨ shower gel	⑩ bathmat	⑪ towel	⑫ toilet
⑬ toilet paper	⑭ mirror				

2 Which colours would you like in your bathroom? ______________________ Colour it.

 Colour and complete the picture to match the sentences.

A red iron is standing on the washing machine.	A black spider is sitting on the wall.	An orange sock is lying on the ground.
A green bottle is standing on the shelf.	A red and a yellow shirt are hanging on the rack.	A pair of blue jeans is hanging over the rack.

Tiger training 2

1 Write the names of the rooms:

bedroom basement bathroom
hall kitchen living room

2 Circle the wrong words.

bathroom: toilet washbasin bathmat mirror bedside table

bedroom: wardrobe desk carpet washing machine bookcase

kitchen: chopping board lamp coffee machine mug toothbrush

Are you afraid of ...

Read the descriptions and write your answers. Mark your answer with a ☒ cross.

... this snake?

Grass snakes are not dangerous for humans.

☐ Yes ☐ No

... this rat?

Rats can spread disease.

☐ Yes ☐ No

... this spider?

Garden spiders are not dangerous for humans.

☐ Yes ☐ No

... this tick?

Ticks can spread disease.

☐ Yes ☐ No

Yes, I am afraid of this rat and this tick because they

____

____

______________________________.

No, I am not afraid of this snake or this spider because they

____

____

______________________________.

Large or small?

1 Which animals are large, which are small? Fill in the right numbers.
Mark your answer with a ☒ cross.

① snake ② polar bear ③ giraffe ④ fox ⑤ ~~elephant~~ ⑥ horse ⑦ donkey ⑧ butterfly

5

☐ large ☐ small ☐ large ☐ small ☐ large ☐ small ☐ large ☐ small

☐ large ☐ small ☐ large ☐ small ☐ large ☐ small ☐ large ☐ small

2 Which animal is the smallest? The smallest animal is the ____________________.

3 Which animal is the largest? ______________________________.

1 Find the words and match with the photos.

sharkrattlesnakepiranhabluepoisondartfrogcaymantarantula

2 Which animals use poison? ______________________________

____

 Write under the pictures.

bear	deer	wild boar	woodpecker	hedgehog	wolf	squirrel	badger

hippo: thirty-eight to forty-two teeth

shark: up to six thousand teeth

piranha: this one has about twenty-six teeth

crocodile: about sixty teeth

pittbull terrier: forty-two teeth

jaguar: thirty teeth

1 Which animal has the largest teeth?

______________________________.

2 Which animal has the most teeth?

______________________________.

lion

lemur

wolf

A Japanese macaque has yellow eyes.

owl

1 Can you guess or do you know: which animals can see in the dark?

______________________________.

2 Which colour are the animals eyes?

______________________________.

3 Which animals live freely in the wild in Germany?

____

______________________________.

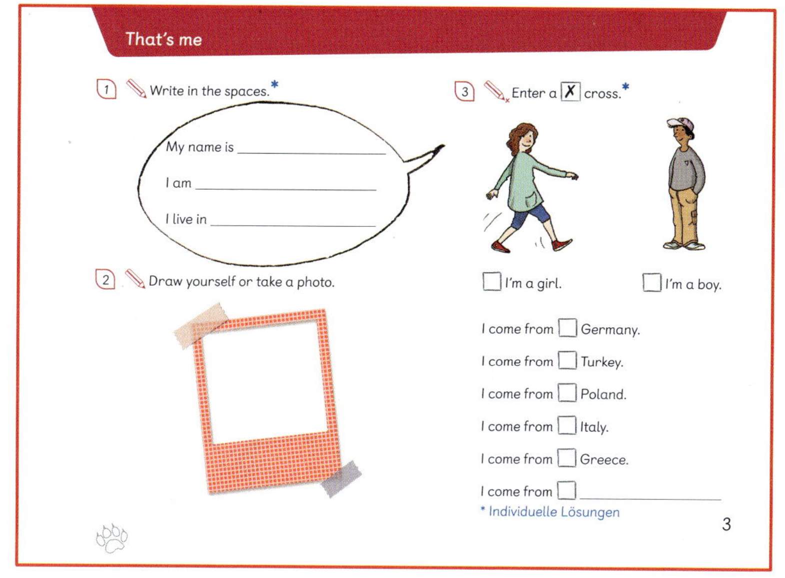

That's me

1 Write in the spaces.*

My name is ____________

I am ____________

I live in ____________

2 Draw yourself or take a photo.

3 Enter a ☒ cross.*

☐ I'm a girl. ☐ I'm a boy.

I come from ☐ Germany.

I come from ☐ Turkey.

I come from ☐ Poland.

I come from ☐ Italy.

I come from ☐ Greece.

I come from ☐ ____________

* Individuelle Lösungen

3

My family

1 Unscramble and write.

r h a t e f — e h m t r o — r o b e h t r — s r e i t s

father — sister

mother — brother

2 Draw your family or take a photo.*

3 Enter a ☒ cross.*

Do you have a sister?	☐ Yes	☐ No
Do you have a brother?	☐ Yes	☐ No
Do you have an aunt?	☐ Yes	☐ No
Do you have an uncle?	☐ Yes	☐ No
Do you have a grandma?	☐ Yes	☐ No
Do you have a grandpa?	☐ Yes	☐ No

I have ☐ ____________

* Individuelle Lösungen

Have a look!

1 Fill in:

~~stars~~ ~~orange~~ ~~stripes~~ ~~guitar~~ ~~blue~~

orange — stars — stripes — guitar — blue

2 Fill in:

~~blonde~~ ~~brown~~ ~~present~~ ~~orange~~ ~~green~~

green — present — orange — blonde — brown

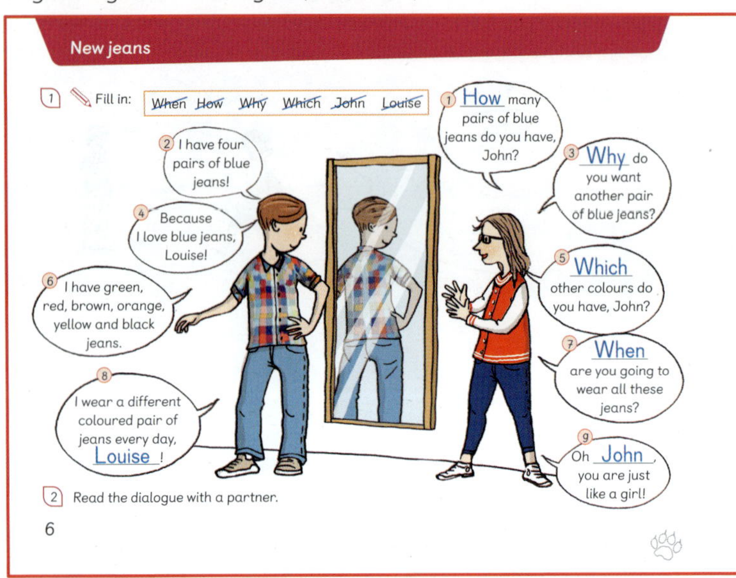
New jeans
1 Fill in: When How Why Which John Louise
1 How many pairs of blue jeans do you have, John?
2 I have four pairs of blue jeans!
3 Why do you want another pair of blue jeans?
4 Because I love blue jeans, Louise!
5 Which other colours do you have, John?
6 I have green, red, brown, orange, yellow and black jeans.
7 When are you going to wear all these jeans?
8 I wear a different coloured pair of jeans every day, Louise!
9 Oh John, you are just like a girl!
2 Read the dialogue with a partner.
6

My hobbies
What do you like to do? Write and mark your answer with a X cross.*
riding a bike
playing computer games
reading a book
swimming in the pool
singing a song
dancing to the music
cooking a meal
writing a story
writing a story
cooking a meal
singing a song
reading a book
swimming in the pool
dancing to the music
playing computer games
riding a bike
* Individuelle Lösungen
7

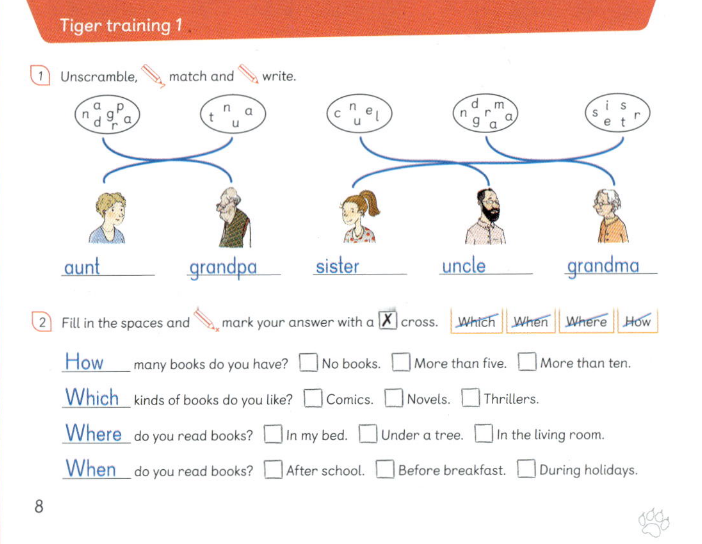
Tiger training 1
1 Unscramble, match and write.
n a d g p r a
t n u a
c n u e l
n d g r m a a
s i e t r
aunt
grandpa
sister
uncle
grandma
2 Fill in the spaces and mark your answer with a X cross. Which When Where How
How many books do you have? No books. More than five. More than ten.
Which kinds of books do you like? Comics. Novels. Thrillers.
Where do you read books? In my bed. Under a tree. In the living room.
When do you read books? After school. Before breakfast. During holidays.
8

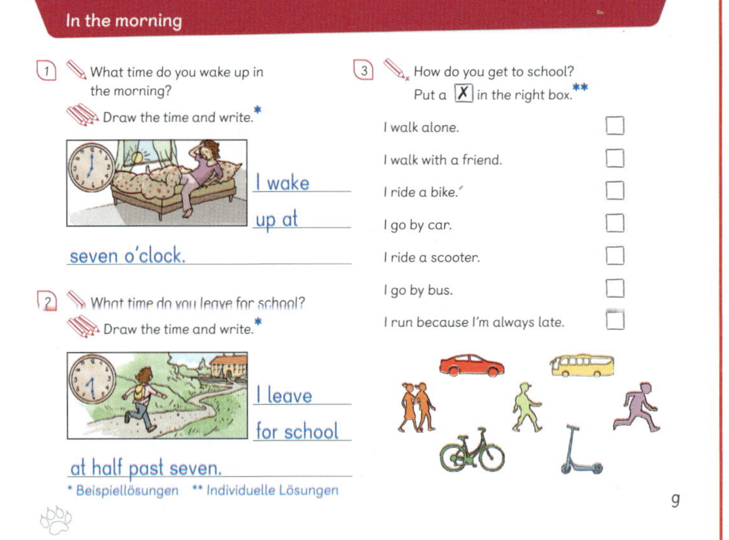
In the morning
1 What time do you wake up in the morning?
Draw the time and write.*
I wake up at seven o'clock.
2 What time do you leave for school?
Draw the time and write.*
I leave for school at half past seven.
* Beispiellösungen ** Individuelle Lösungen
3 How do you get to school? Put a X in the right box.**
I walk alone.
I walk with a friend.
I ride a bike.
I go by car.
I ride a scooter.
I go by bus.
I run because I'm always late.
9

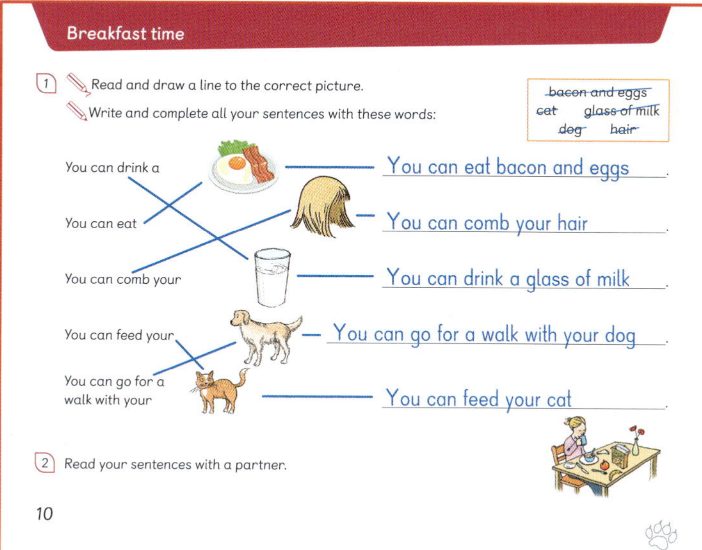
Breakfast time
1 Read and draw a line to the correct picture.
Write and complete all your sentences with these words:
bacon and eggs
cat glass of milk
dog hair
You can drink a
You can eat
You can comb your
You can feed your
You can go for a walk with your
You can eat bacon and eggs.
You can comb your hair.
You can drink a glass of milk.
You can go for a walk with your dog.
You can feed your cat.
2 Read your sentences with a partner.
10

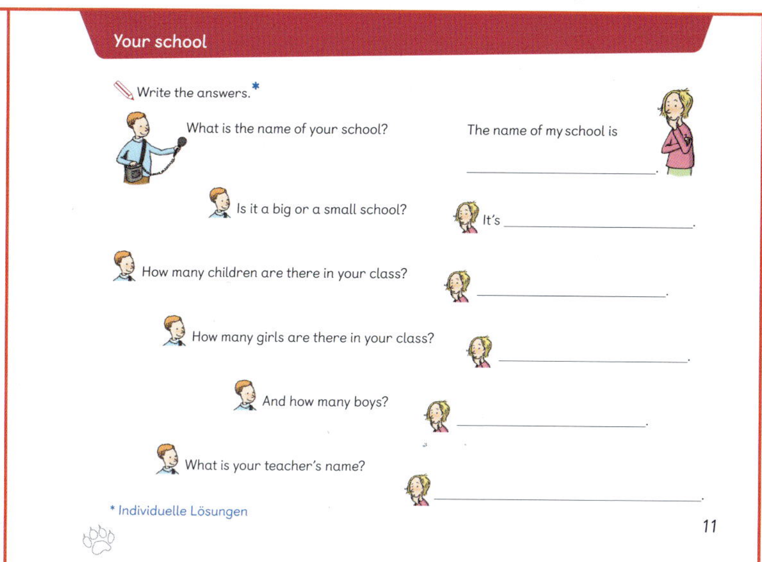
Your school
Write the answers.*
What is the name of your school?
The name of my school is
Is it a big or a small school?
It's
How many children are there in your class?
How many girls are there in your class?
And how many boys?
What is your teacher's name?
* Individuelle Lösungen
11

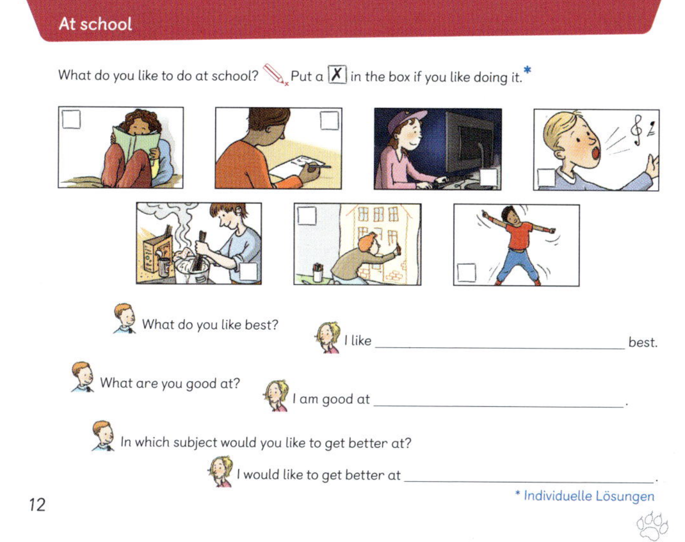
At school
What do you like to do at school? Put a ☒ in the box if you like doing it.*
What do you like best?
I like best.
What are you good at?
I am good at
In which subject would you like to get better at?
I would like to get better at
* Individuelle Lösungen
12

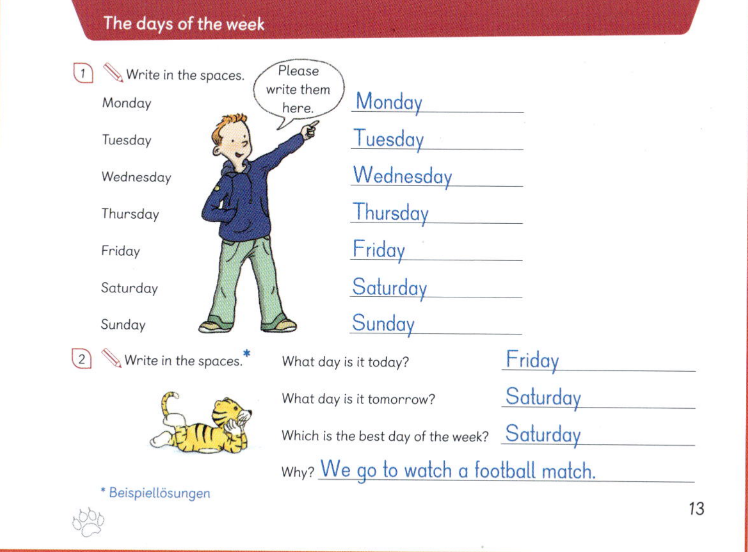
The days of the week
1 Write in the spaces.
Please write them here.
Monday
Tuesday
Wednesday
Thursday
Friday
Saturday
Sunday
Monday
Tuesday
Wednesday
Thursday
Friday
Saturday
Sunday
2 Write in the spaces.*
What day is it today? Friday
What day is it tomorrow? Saturday
Which is the best day of the week? Saturday
Why? We go to watch a football match.
* Beispiellösungen
13

Plans for the week

What can Indira and Alex do this week? Write in the spaces.*

~~ride a bike~~ | ~~watch a movie~~ | ~~play football~~ | ~~ride a horse~~ | ~~tidy your room~~ | ~~play badminton~~ | ~~go for a picnic~~

On Monday we can ride a bike.

On Tuesday we can watch a movie.

On Wednesday we can play football.

On Thursday we can tidy your room.

On Friday we can ride a horse.

On Saturday we can play badminton.

On Sunday we can go for a picnic.

* Beispiellösungen

What do they love doing?

Complete the sentences to the pictures:

~~...loves dancing.~~ | ~~...loves fishing.~~ | ~~loves playing football.~~ | ~~...loves swimming.~~

Mary loves playing football.

Luke loves swimming.

Lara loves dancing.

Alex loves fishing.

What do you love doing?* I love horse riding.

What does your best friend love doing?* She loves skateboarding.

* Beispiellösungen

How well do you know your best friend?

1 Think for a little while and enter a [X] cross.*

2 [X] And now your friend!*

Does he/she	Yes	No	Yes	No
play cards?	☐	☐	☐	☐
play chess?	☐	☐	☐	☐
play football?	☐	☐	☐	☐
make biscuits?	☐	☐	☐	☐
write letters?	☐	☐	☐	☐
______ *	☐	☐	☐	☐

3 Compare your answers with those of your friend.*

How many same answers do you have? ______

* Individuelle Lösungen

Would you like to ...

What would you like to do?*

Yes, I would. | No, I wouldn't.

Would you like to go up in a balloon? Yes, I would.

Would you like to sky dive? No, I wouldn't.

Would you like to be a successful author? Yes, I would.

Would you like to swim with dolphins? No, I wouldn't.

Would you like to be a famous musician? Yes, I would.

* Beispiellösungen

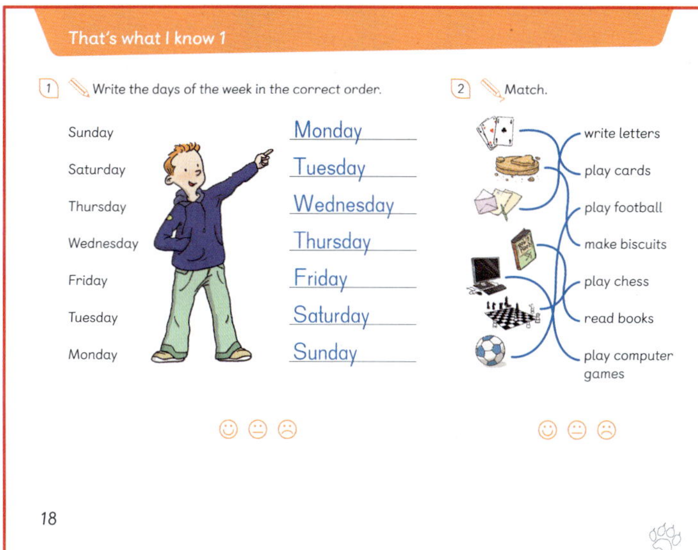

That's what I know 1

1 Write the days of the week in the correct order.

Sunday	Monday
Saturday	Tuesday
Thursday	Wednesday
Wednesday	Thursday
Friday	Friday
Tuesday	Saturday
Monday	Sunday

2 Match.

- write letters
- play cards
- play football
- make biscuits
- play chess
- read books
- play computer games

18

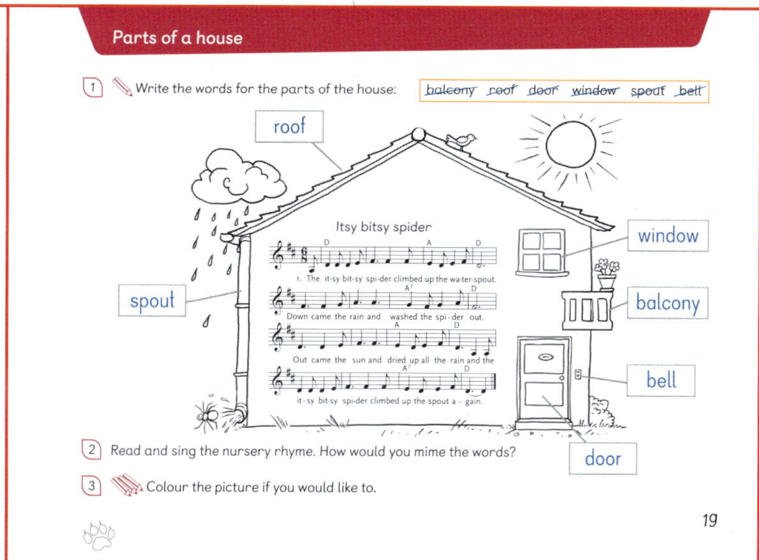

Parts of a house

1 Write the words for the parts of the house: ~~balcony~~ ~~roof~~ ~~door~~ ~~window~~ ~~spout~~ ~~bell~~

2 Read and sing the nursery rhyme. How would you mime the words?

3 Colour the picture if you would like to.

19

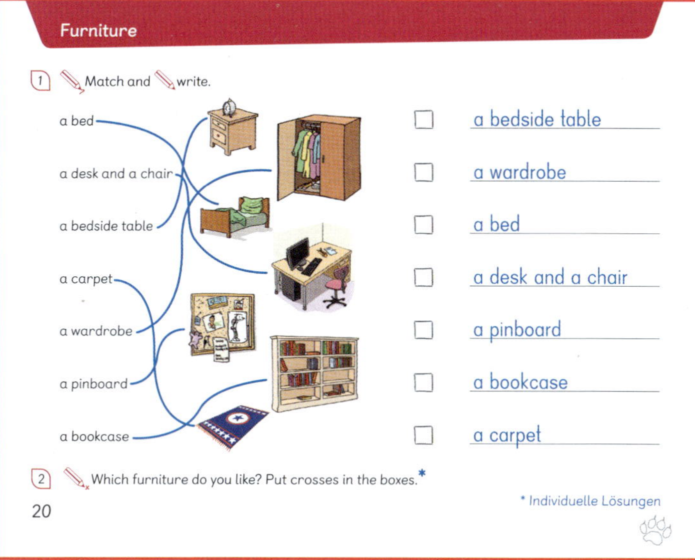

Furniture

1 Match and write.

a bed	☐ a bedside table
a desk and a chair	☐ a wardrobe
a bedside table	☐ a bed
a carpet	☐ a desk and a chair
a wardrobe	☐ a pinboard
a pinboard	☐ a bookcase
a bookcase	☐ a carpet

2 Which furniture do you like? Put crosses in the boxes.*

* Individuelle Lösungen

20

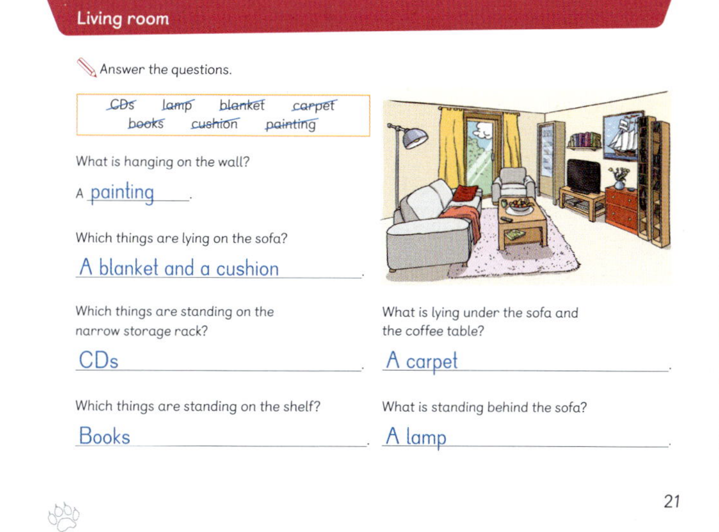

Living room

Answer the questions.

~~CDs~~ ~~lamp~~ ~~blanket~~ ~~carpet~~ ~~books~~ ~~cushion~~ ~~painting~~

What is hanging on the wall?
A painting.

Which things are lying on the sofa?
A blanket and a cushion.

Which things are standing on the narrow storage rack?
CDs.

What is lying under the sofa and the coffee table?
A carpet.

Which things are standing on the shelf?
Books.

What is standing behind the sofa?
A lamp.

21

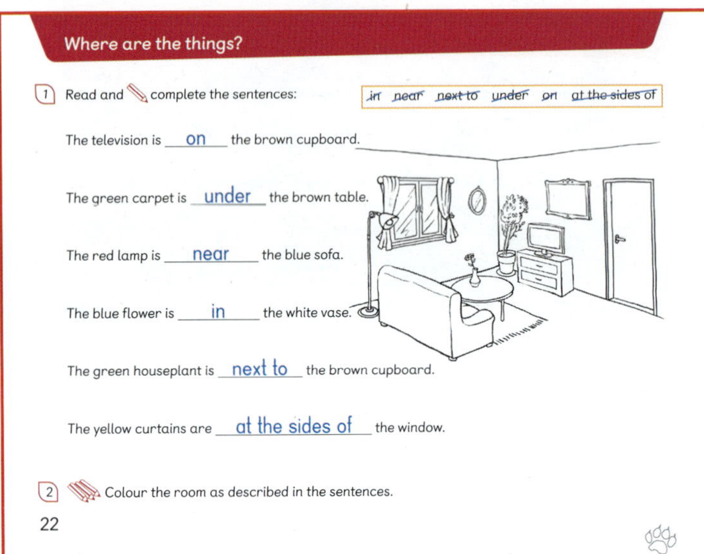

Where are the things?

1 Read and complete the sentences: ~~in~~ ~~near~~ ~~next to~~ ~~under~~ ~~on~~ ~~at the sides of~~

The television is __on__ the brown cupboard.

The green carpet is __under__ the brown table.

The red lamp is __near__ the blue sofa.

The blue flower is __in__ the white vase.

The green houseplant is __next to__ the brown cupboard.

The yellow curtains are __at the sides of__ the window.

2 Colour the room as described in the sentences.

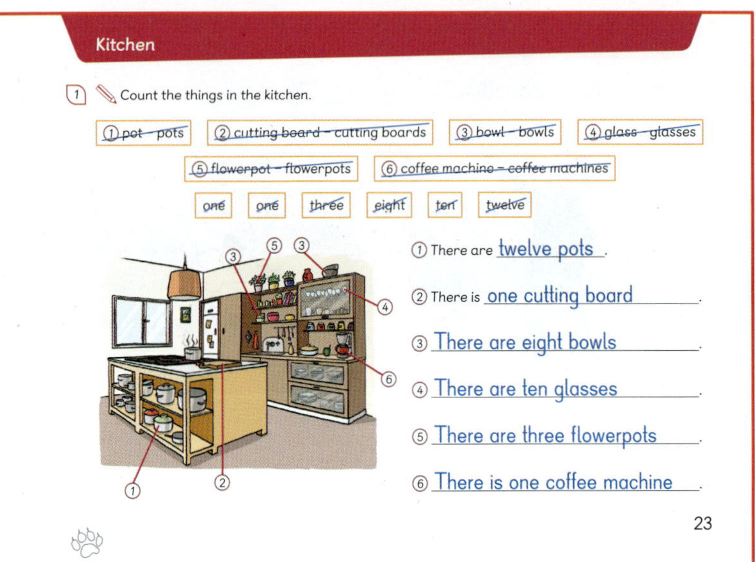

Kitchen

1 Count the things in the kitchen.

① ~~pot – pots~~ ② ~~cutting board – cutting boards~~ ③ ~~bowl – bowls~~ ④ ~~glass – glasses~~ ⑤ ~~flowerpot – flowerpots~~ ⑥ ~~coffee machine – coffee machines~~

~~one~~ ~~one~~ ~~three~~ ~~eight~~ ~~ten~~ ~~twelve~~

① There are __twelve pots__.

② There is __one cutting board__.

③ __There are eight bowls__.

④ __There are ten glasses__.

⑤ __There are three flowerpots__.

⑥ __There is one coffee machine__.

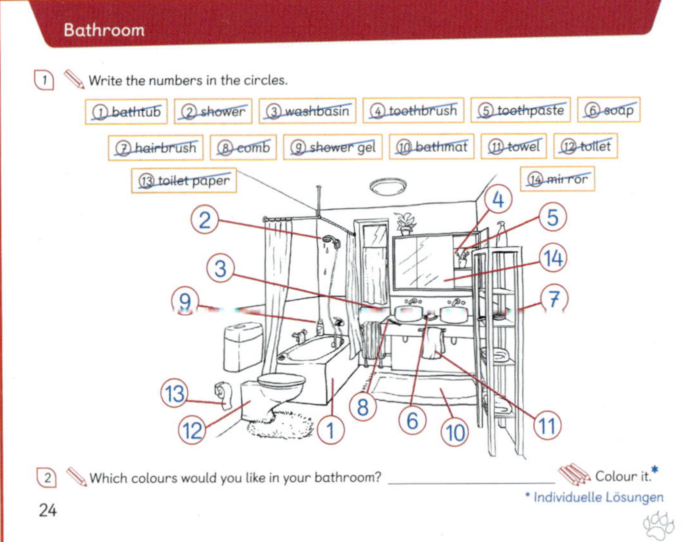

Bathroom

1 Write the numbers in the circles.

~~① bathtub~~ ~~② shower~~ ~~③ washbasin~~ ~~④ toothbrush~~ ~~⑤ toothpaste~~ ~~⑥ soap~~ ~~⑦ hairbrush~~ ~~⑧ comb~~ ~~⑨ shower gel~~ ~~⑩ bathmat~~ ~~⑪ towel~~ ~~⑫ toilet~~ ~~⑬ toilet paper~~ ~~⑭ mirror~~

2 Which colours would you like in your bathroom? ______ Colour it.*

* Individuelle Lösungen

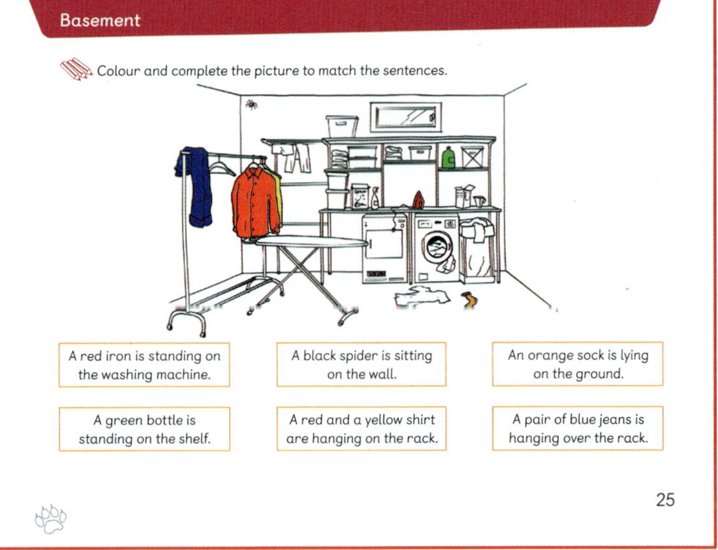

Basement

Colour and complete the picture to match the sentences.

A red iron is standing on the washing machine.	A black spider is sitting on the wall.	An orange sock is lying on the ground.
A green bottle is standing on the shelf.	A red and a yellow shirt are hanging on the rack.	A pair of blue jeans is hanging over the rack.

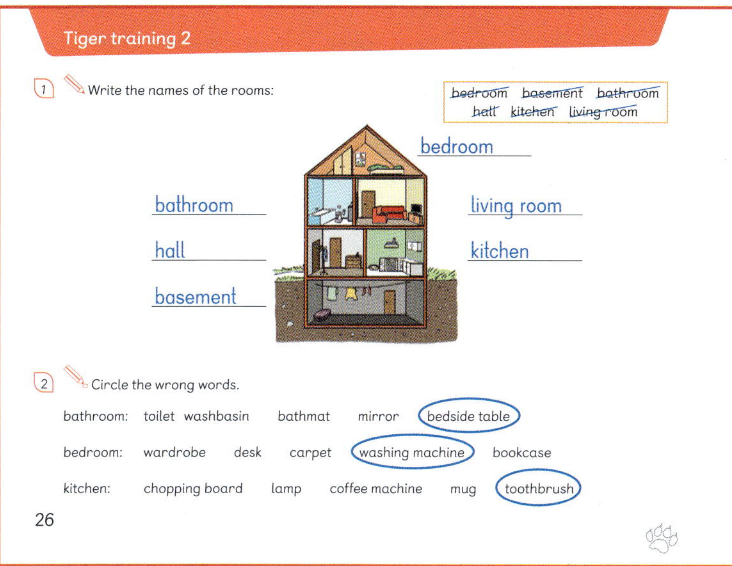

Tiger training 2

1 Write the names of the rooms:

~~bedroom~~ ~~basement~~ ~~bathroom~~ ~~hall~~ ~~kitchen~~ ~~living room~~

bedroom

bathroom

living room

hall

kitchen

basement

2 Circle the wrong words.

bathroom: toilet washbasin bathmat mirror (bedside table)

bedroom: wardrobe desk carpet (washing machine) bookcase

kitchen: chopping board lamp coffee machine mug (toothbrush)

26

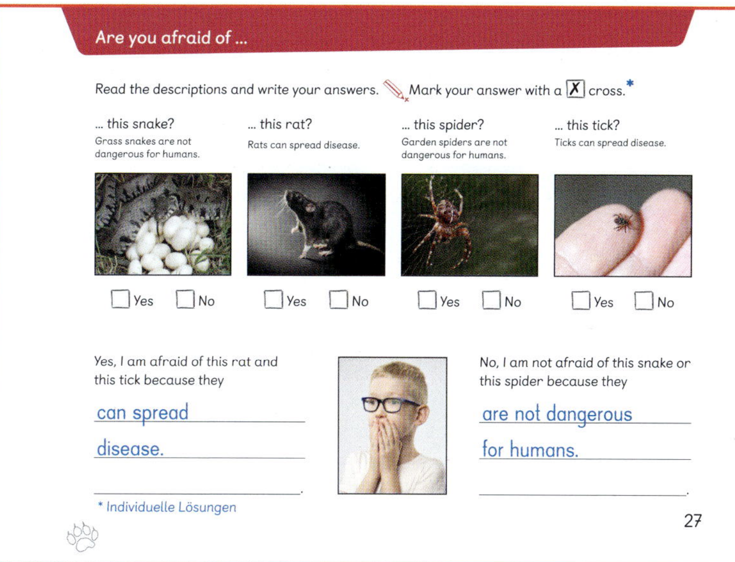

Are you afraid of ...

Read the descriptions and write your answers. Mark your answer with a ☒ cross.*

... this snake? Grass snakes are not dangerous for humans.

... this rat? Rats can spread disease.

... this spider? Garden spiders are not dangerous for humans.

... this tick? Ticks can spread disease.

☐ Yes ☐ No ☐ Yes ☐ No ☐ Yes ☐ No ☐ Yes ☐ No

Yes, I am afraid of this rat and this tick because they can spread disease.

No, I am not afraid of this snake or this spider because they are not dangerous for humans.

* Individuelle Lösungen

27

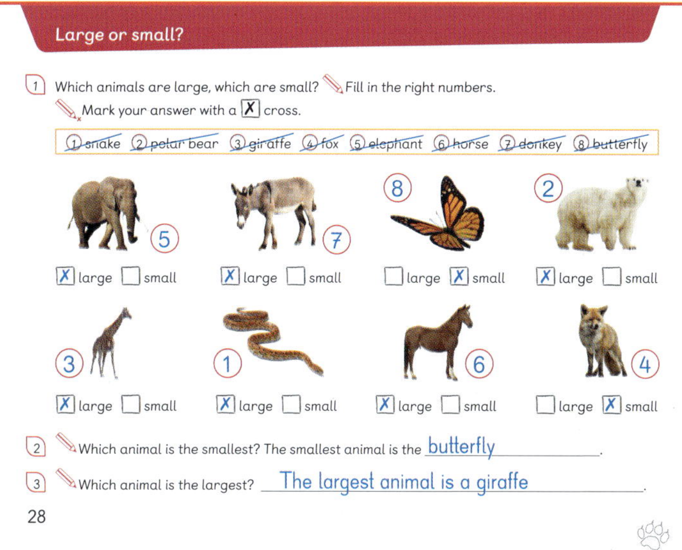

Large or small?

1 Which animals are large, which are small? Fill in the right numbers. Mark your answer with a ☒ cross.

~~1 snake~~ ~~2 polar bear~~ ~~3 giraffe~~ ~~4 fox~~ ~~5 elephant~~ ~~6 horse~~ ~~7 donkey~~ ~~8 butterfly~~

5 ☒ large ☐ small | 7 ☒ large ☐ small | 8 ☐ large ☒ small | 2 ☒ large ☐ small

3 ☒ large ☐ small | 1 ☒ large ☐ small | 6 ☒ large ☐ small | 4 ☐ large ☒ small

2 Which animal is the smallest? The smallest animal is the butterfly.

3 Which animal is the largest? The largest animal is a giraffe.

28

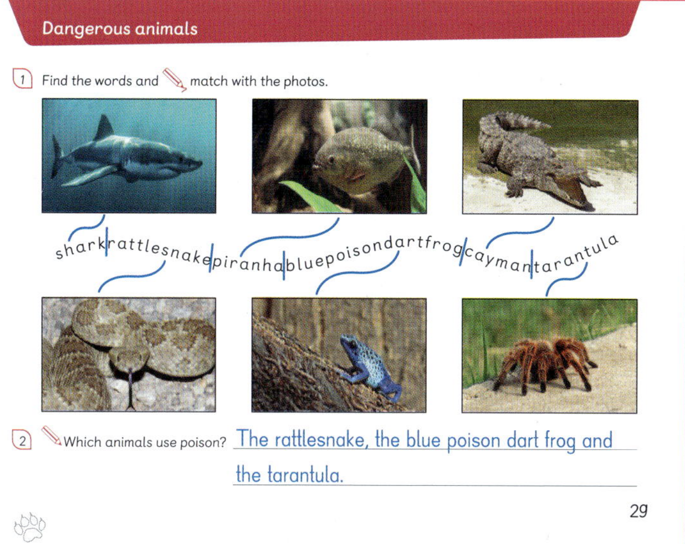

Dangerous animals

1 Find the words and match with the photos.

shark|rattlesnake|piranha|bluepoisondartfrog|cayman|tarantula

2 Which animals use poison? The rattlesnake, the blue poison dart frog and the tarantula.

29

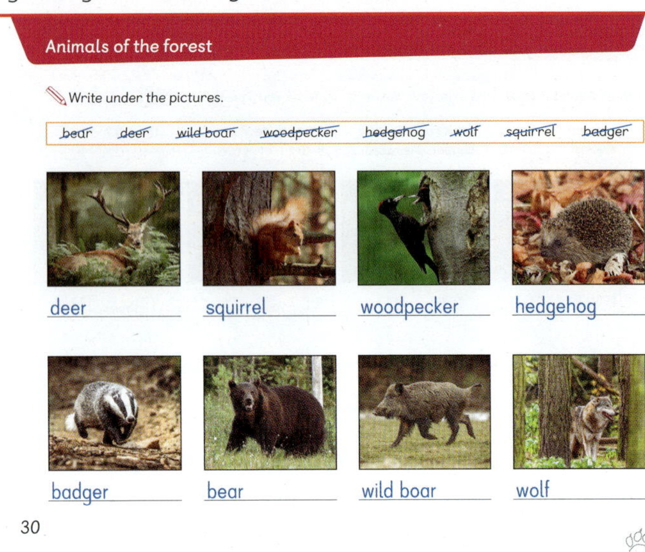

Animals of the forest

Write under the pictures.

~~bear~~ ~~deer~~ ~~wild boar~~ ~~woodpecker~~ ~~hedgehog~~ ~~wolf~~ ~~squirrel~~ ~~badger~~

deer | squirrel | woodpecker | hedgehog

badger | bear | wild boar | wolf

30

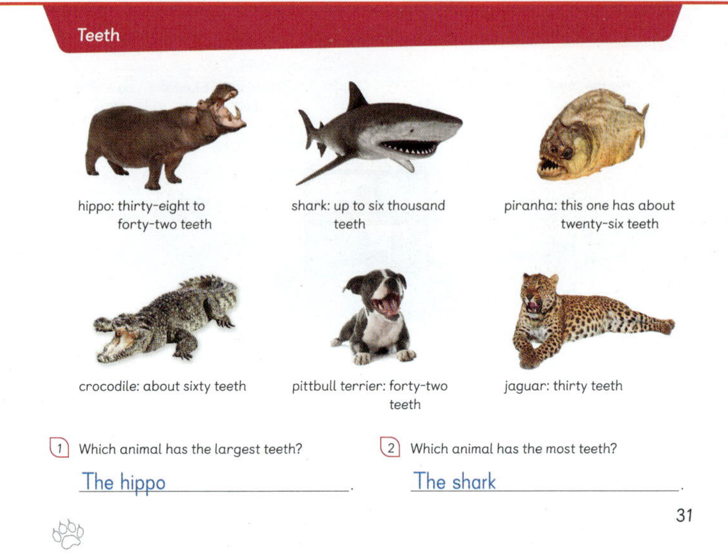

Teeth

hippo: thirty-eight to forty-two teeth

shark: up to six thousand teeth

piranha: this one has about twenty-six teeth

crocodile: about sixty teeth

pittbull terrier: forty-two teeth

jaguar: thirty teeth

1 Which animal has the largest teeth?

The hippo.

2 Which animal has the most teeth?

The shark.

31

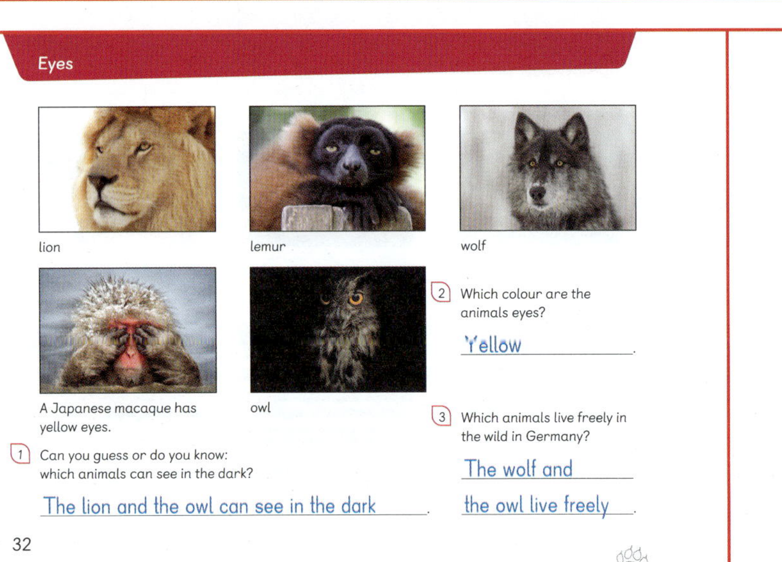

Eyes

lion

lemur

wolf

A Japanese macaque has yellow eyes.

owl

1 Can you guess or do you know: which animals can see in the dark?

The lion and the owl can see in the dark.

2 Which colour are the animals eyes?

Yellow.

3 Which animals live freely in the wild in Germany?

The wolf and the owl live freely.

32

Animal tracks

Circle the animal tracks as the animals in the same colour.

cat, hippo, leopard, cheetah, otter, fox

impala, coyote, elephant, lion, rhino, hare

rabbit, racoon, beaver, bear, opossum, weasel

muskrat, deer, cow, moose, dog, squirrel

33

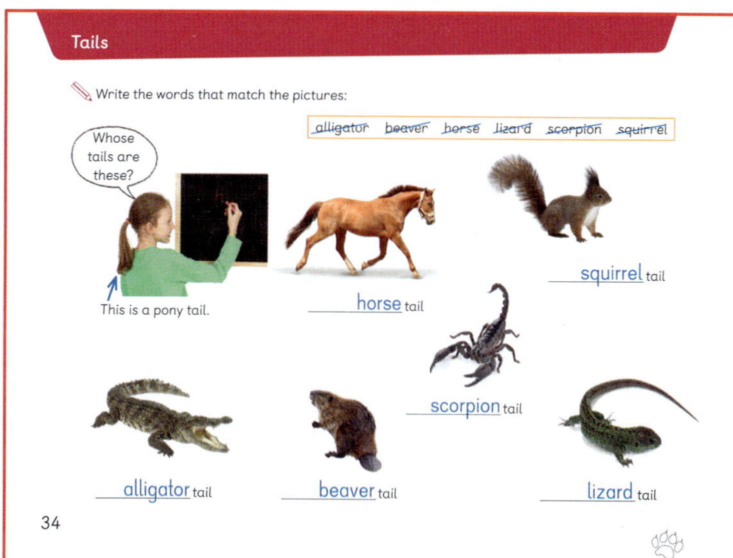

Tails

Write the words that match the pictures:

~~alligator~~ ~~beaver~~ ~~horse~~ ~~lizard~~ ~~scorpion~~ ~~squirrel~~

Whose tails are these?

This is a pony tail.

horse tail

squirrel tail

scorpion tail

alligator tail

beaver tail

lizard tail

34

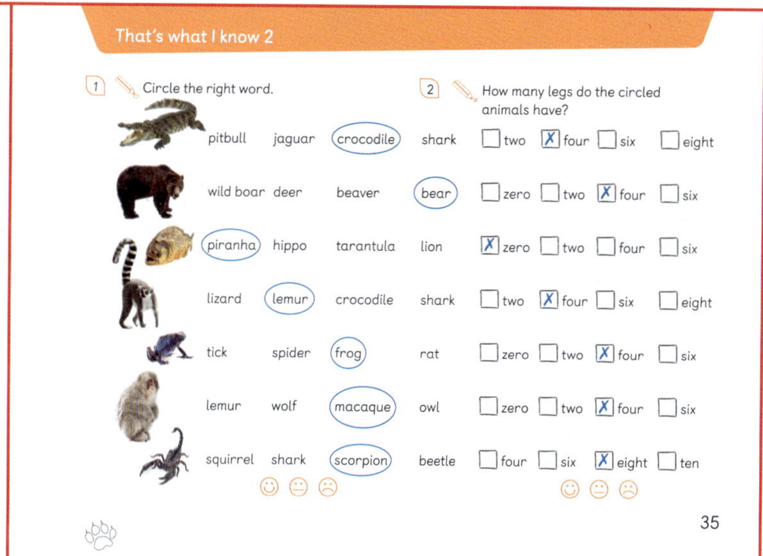

That's what I know 2

1 Circle the right word.

2 How many legs do the circled animals have?

pitbull	jaguar	**(crocodile)**	shark	☐ two	☒ four	☐ six	☐ eight
wild boar	deer	beaver	**(bear)**	☐ zero	☐ two	☒ four	☐ six
(piranha)	hippo	tarantula	lion	☒ zero	☐ two	☐ four	☐ six
lizard	**(lemur)**	crocodile	shark	☐ two	☒ four	☐ six	☐ eight
tick	spider	**(frog)**	rat	☐ zero	☐ two	☒ four	☐ six
lemur	wolf	**(macaque)**	owl	☐ zero	☐ two	☒ four	☐ six
squirrel	shark	**(scorpion)**	beetle	☐ four	☐ six	☒ eight	☐ ten

35

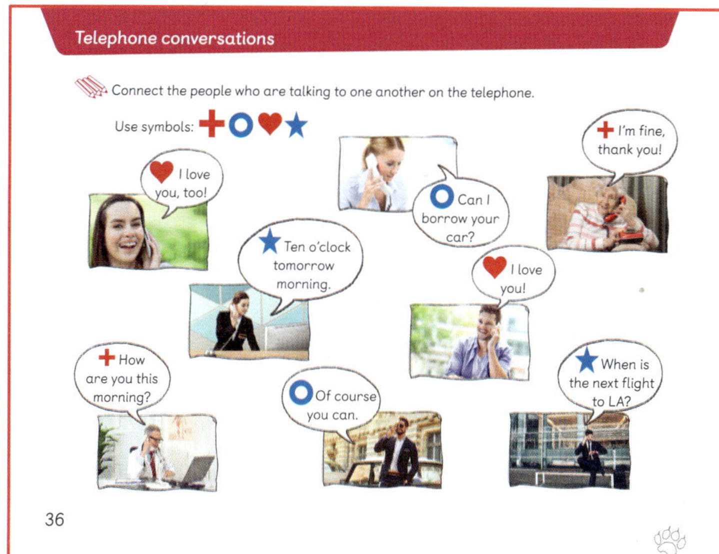

Telephone conversations

Connect the people who are talking to one another on the telephone.

Use symbols: ✚ ○ ♥ ★

36

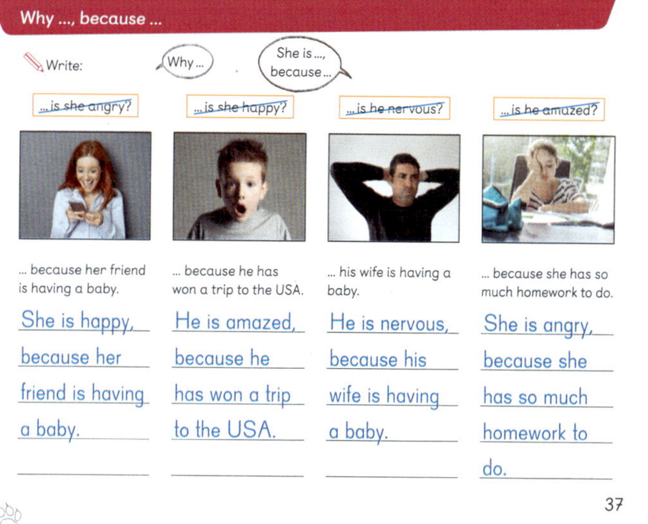

Why ..., because ...

Write:

~~... is she angry?~~	~~... is she happy?~~	~~... is he nervous?~~	~~... is he amazed?~~
... because her friend is having a baby.	... because he has won a trip to the USA.	... his wife is having a baby.	... because she has so much homework to do.
She is happy, because her friend is having a baby.	He is amazed, because he has won a trip to the USA.	He is nervous, because his wife is having a baby.	She is angry, because she has so much homework to do.

37

Feelings
My meal is tasteless.
That looks really good.
envious
happy
Write:
happy
envious
envious
tired
angry
nervous
happy
tired
nervous
angry
envious
happy
38

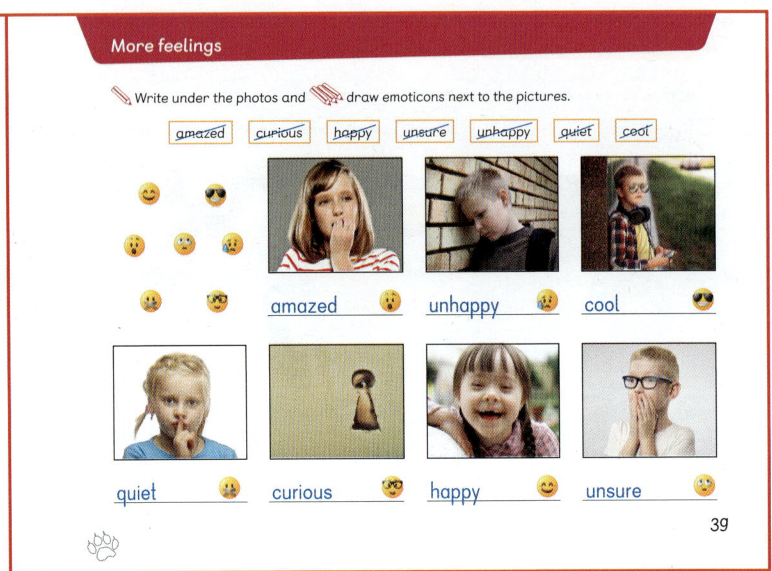
More feelings
Write under the photos and draw emoticons next to the pictures.
amazed
curious
happy
unsure
unhappy
quiet
cool
amazed
unhappy
cool
quiet
curious
happy
unsure
39

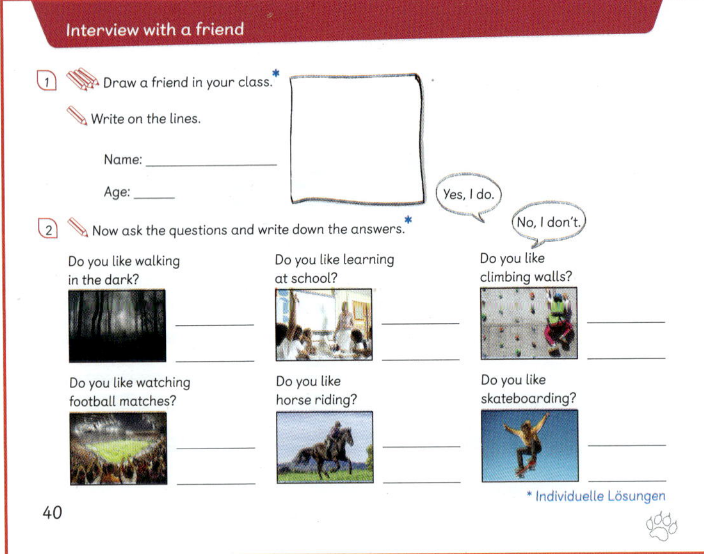
Interview with a friend
1 Draw a friend in your class.*
Write on the lines.
Name:
Age:
2 Now ask the questions and write down the answers.*
Yes, I do.
No, I don't.
Do you like walking in the dark?
Do you like learning at school?
Do you like climbing walls?
Do you like watching football matches?
Do you like horse riding?
Do you like skateboarding?
* Individuelle Lösungen
40

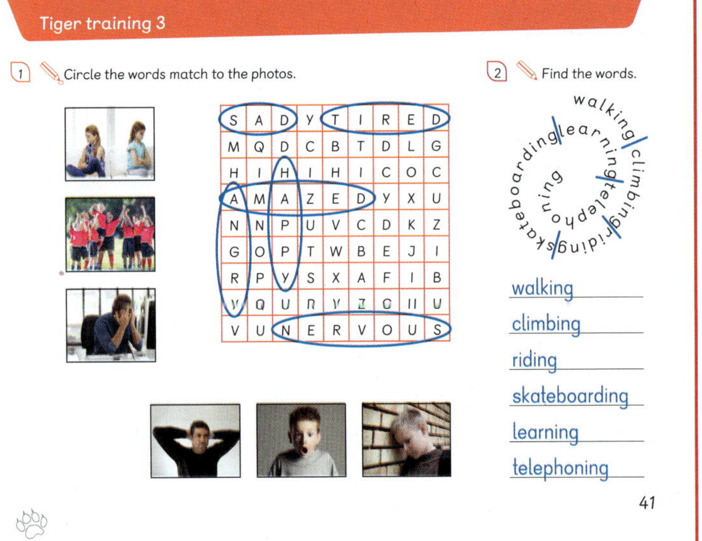
Tiger training 3
1 Circle the words match to the photos.
S A D Y T I R E D
M Q D C B T D L G
H I H I H I C O C
A M A Z E D Y X U
N N P U V C D K Z
G O P T W B E J I
R P Y S X A F I B
Y Q U R Y Z G H U
V U N E R V O U S
2 Find the words.
walking
climbing
riding
skateboarding
learning
telephoning
41

Let's cook!

Write a shopping list for a delicious meal.
Choose chilli con carne or spaghetti bolognese.*

spaghetti rice beans onions tomatoes garlic oregano
sweet pepper pepper salt minced meat ketchup

Shopping List:
spaghetti, onions, tomatoes, ketchup, sweet pepper, salt, oregano, pepper, minced meat, garlic

rice, beans, onions, tomatoes, garlic, paprika, pepper, salt, minced meat, ketchup

* Individuelle Lösungen

42

At the sports shop

Fill in the numbers and answer the questions.*

① racket ② basketball ③ bike ④ riding helmet ⑤ inliner ⑥ basket
⑦ football ⑧ waveboard ⑨ hula hoop mature

What sport would you like to do? I would like to play basketball.

What would you like to buy at the sports shop? I would like to buy a basket.

Are you a fan of a certain sport star? I am a fan of Dirk Nowitzky.

* Beispiellösungen

43

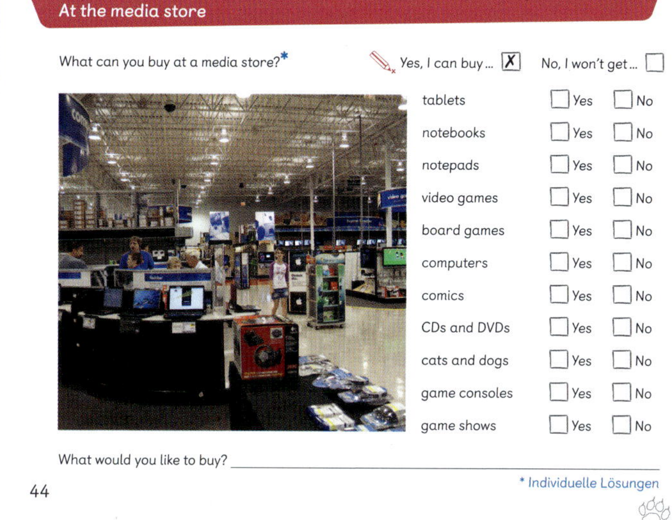

At the media store

What can you buy at a media store?*

Yes, I can buy ... ☒ No, I won't get ... ☐

tablets	☐ Yes	☐ No
notebooks	☐ Yes	☐ No
notepads	☐ Yes	☐ No
video games	☐ Yes	☐ No
board games	☐ Yes	☐ No
computers	☐ Yes	☐ No
comics	☐ Yes	☐ No
CDs and DVDs	☐ Yes	☐ No
cats and dogs	☐ Yes	☐ No
game consoles	☐ Yes	☐ No
game shows	☐ Yes	☐ No

What would you like to buy? ______

* Individuelle Lösungen

44

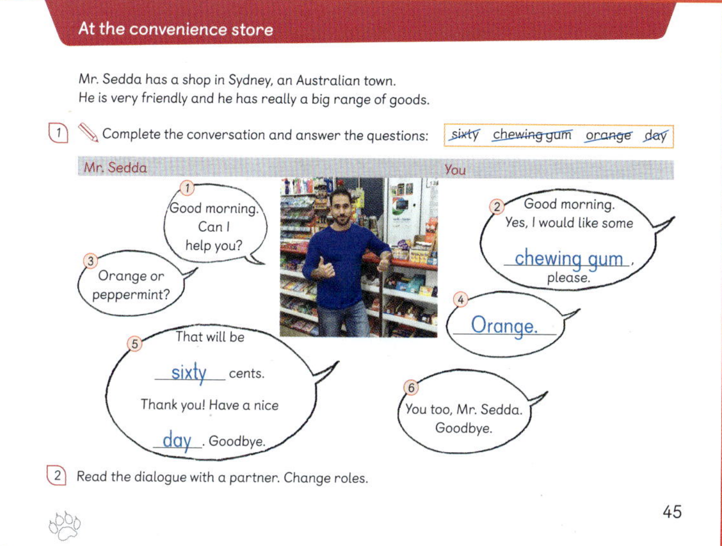

At the convenience store

Mr. Sedda has a shop in Sydney, an Australian town.
He is very friendly and he has really a big range of goods.

1 Complete the conversation and answer the questions: sixty chewing gum orange day

Mr. Sedda / You

1. Good morning. Can I help you?
2. Good morning. Yes, I would like some chewing gum, please.
3. Orange or peppermint?
4. Orange.
5. That will be sixty cents. Thank you! Have a nice day. Goodbye.
6. You too, Mr. Sedda. Goodbye.

2 Read the dialogue with a partner. Change roles.

45

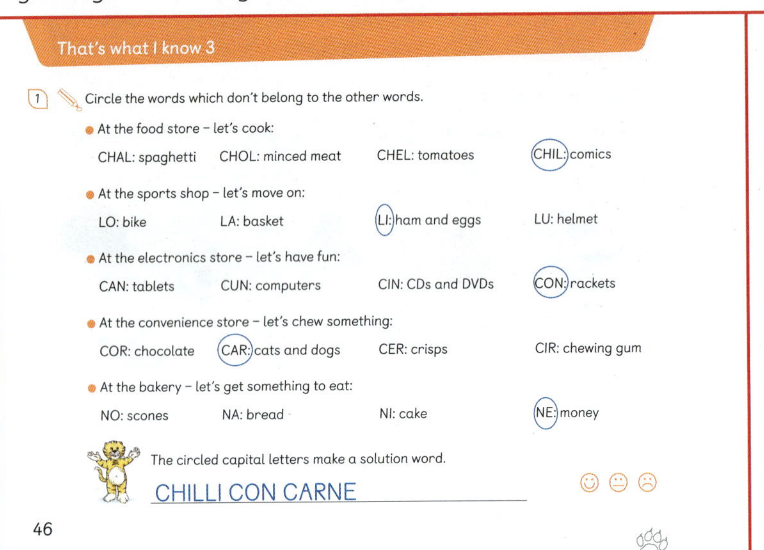

That's what I know 3

1 Circle the words which don't belong to the other words.

- At the food store – let's cook:
  CHAL: spaghetti CHOL: minced meat CHEL: tomatoes (CHIL:) comics
- At the sports shop – let's move on:
  LO: bike LA: basket (LI:) ham and eggs LU: helmet
- At the electronics store – let's have fun:
  CAN: tablets CUN: computers CIN: CDs and DVDs (CON:) rackets
- At the convenience store – let's chew something:
  COR: chocolate (CAR:) cats and dogs CER: crisps CIR: chewing gum
- At the bakery – let's get something to eat:
  NO: scones NA: bread NI: cake (NE:) money

The circled capital letters make a solution word.

CHILLI CON CARNE

46

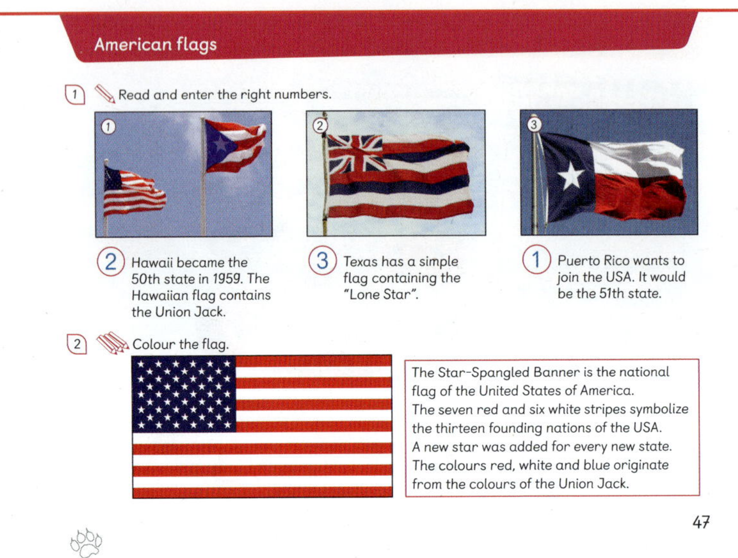

American flags

1 Read and enter the right numbers.

(2) Hawaii became the 50th state in 1959. The Hawaiian flag contains the Union Jack.

(3) Texas has a simple flag containing the "Lone Star".

(1) Puerto Rico wants to join the USA. It would be the 51th state.

2 Colour the flag.

The Star-Spangled Banner is the national flag of the United States of America.
The seven red and six white stripes symbolize the thirteen founding nations of the USA.
A new star was added for every new state.
The colours red, white and blue originate from the colours of the Union Jack.

47

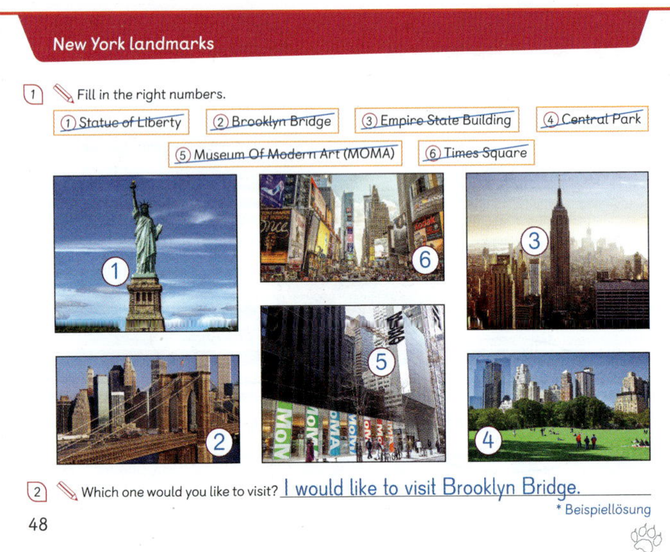

New York landmarks

1 Fill in the right numbers.

1 Statue of Liberty 2 Brooklyn Bridge 3 Empire State Building 4 Central Park 5 Museum Of Modern Art (MOMA) 6 Times Square

2 Which one would you like to visit? I would like to visit Brooklyn Bridge.

* Beispiellösung

48

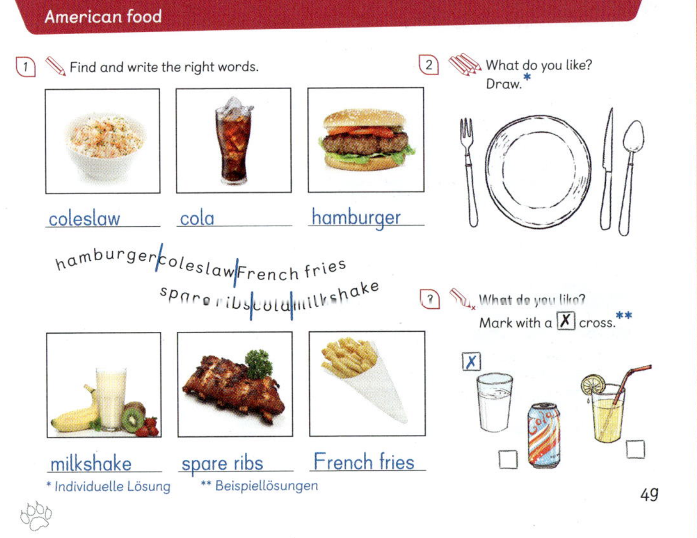

American food

1 Find and write the right words.

coleslaw cola hamburger

hamburger|coleslaw|French fries
spare ribs|cola|milkshake

milkshake spare ribs French fries

2 What do you like? Draw.*

? What do you like? Mark with a [X] cross.**

* Individuelle Lösung ** Beispiellösungen

49

NBA: Basketball

Read. Enter the right numbers.

1	backboard	vertical board with a basket attached
2	basket	the basket is a steel rim with a net attached to it
3	court	in international games 28 meters long and 15 meters wide
4	basketball	equipment
5	jersey	sport clothes
6	high-tops	shoes

Guy on the left: Dirk Nowitzki is a German basketball player for the Dallas Mavericks in the National Basketball Association (NBA). He is the highest-scoring non-American player in NBA history and the sixth player to achieve over 30,000 regular season points.

Guy on the right: Dennis Schroeder is a German basketball player for the Atlanta Hawks in the NBA. He formerly played for SG Braunschweig and Phantoms Braunschweig. He is widely regarded as one of the best talents in German basketball.

A popular American President

Enter the numbers and sing the anthem.

1 Barack Obama was the first black US President.
2 He is married to Michelle Obama.
3 They have two children: Malia Ann and Natasha.
4 The President of the United States lives in the White House in Washington, D. C.

American currency

1 How much is it?

88 $

91 ¢

1 half dollar ($)
1 quarter dollar ($)
1 cent ($)
1 dime ($)
5 cents ($)
1 dollar ($)
2 dollars ($)
5 dollars ($)
10 dollars ($)
50 dollars ($)
20 dollars ($)

2 How much money do you need?*

	A junior ticket: $ 26.50	A visit: $ 14.00	A portion: $ 3.00
	I		
	I	IIII	I
			I
	I		
	II	I	

* Beispiellösungen

Tiger training 4

1 Colour the months and special days.

Merry Xmas · spring · January · Happy New Year · July · winter · Easter · October · autumn · April · summer · Happy Halloween

2 Find the months in the circle.

Which is your birthday month?*

* Individuelle Lösung

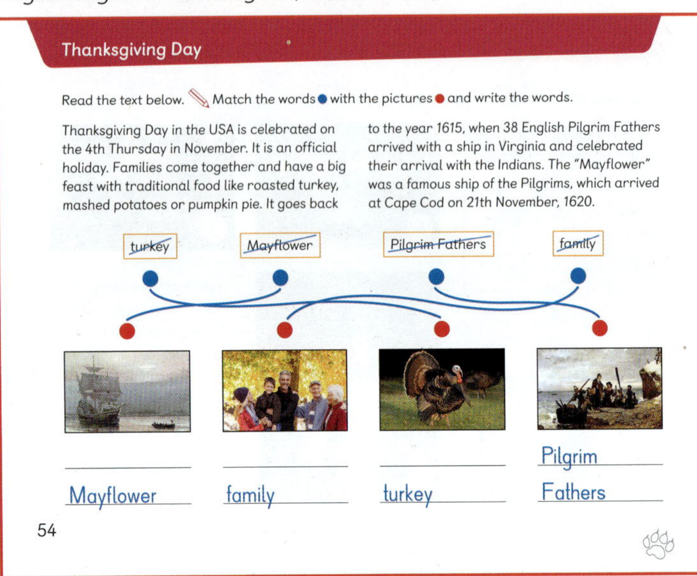

Thanksgiving Day

Read the text below. Match the words with the pictures and write the words.

Thanksgiving Day in the USA is celebrated on the 4th Thursday in November. It is an official holiday. Families come together and have a big feast with traditional food like roasted turkey, mashed potatoes or pumpkin pie. It goes back to the year 1615, when 38 English Pilgrim Fathers arrived with a ship in Virginia and celebrated their arrival with the Indians. The "Mayflower" was a famous ship of the Pilgrims, which arrived at Cape Cod on 21th November, 1620.

~~turkey~~ ~~Mayflower~~ ~~Pilgrim Fathers~~ ~~family~~

Mayflower | family | turkey | Pilgrim Fathers

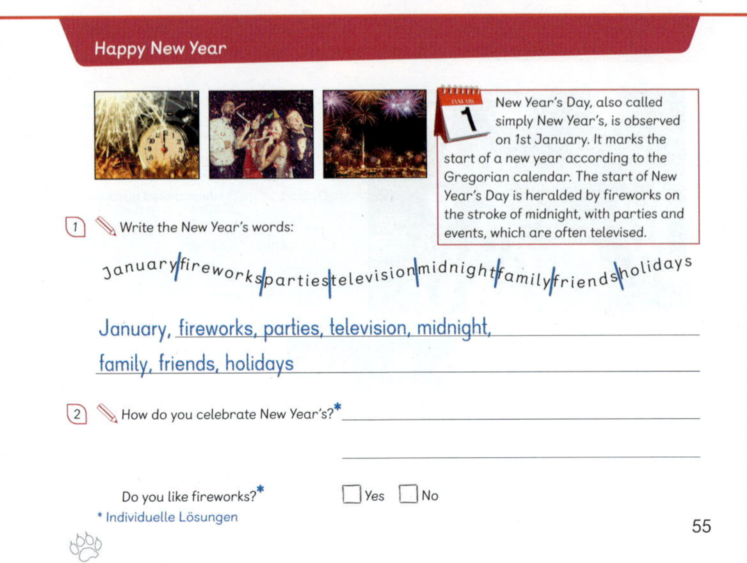

Happy New Year

New Year's Day, also called simply New Year's, is observed on 1st January. It marks the start of a new year according to the Gregorian calendar. The start of New Year's Day is heralded by fireworks on the stroke of midnight, with parties and events, which are often televised.

1. Write the New Year's words:

januaryfireworkspartiestelevisionmidnightfamilyfriendsholidays

January, fireworks, parties, television, midnight, family, friends, holidays

2. How do you celebrate New Year's?*

Do you like fireworks?* ☐ Yes ☐ No

* Individuelle Lösungen

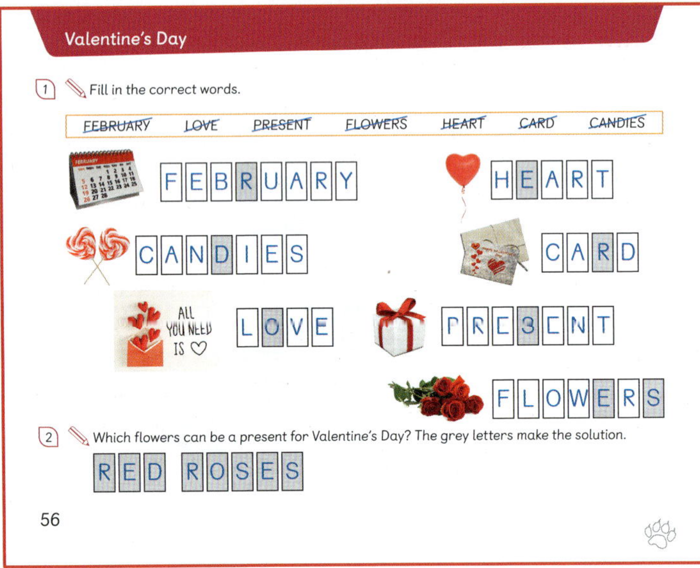

Valentine's Day

1. Fill in the correct words.

~~FEBRUARY~~ ~~LOVE~~ ~~PRESENT~~ ~~FLOWERS~~ ~~HEART~~ ~~CARD~~ ~~CANDIES~~

FEBRUARY | HEART | CANDIES | CARD | LOVE | PRESENT | FLOWERS

2. Which flowers can be a present for Valentine's Day? The grey letters make the solution.

RED ROSES

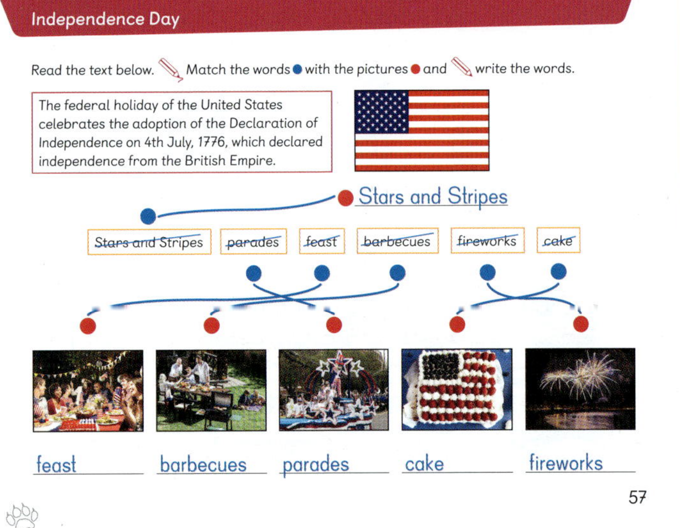

Independence Day

Read the text below. Match the words with the pictures and write the words.

The federal holiday of the United States celebrates the adoption of the Declaration of Independence on 4th July, 1776, which declared independence from the British Empire.

Stars and Stripes

~~Stars and Stripes~~ ~~parades~~ ~~feast~~ ~~barbecues~~ ~~fireworks~~ ~~cake~~

feast | barbecues | parades | cake | fireworks

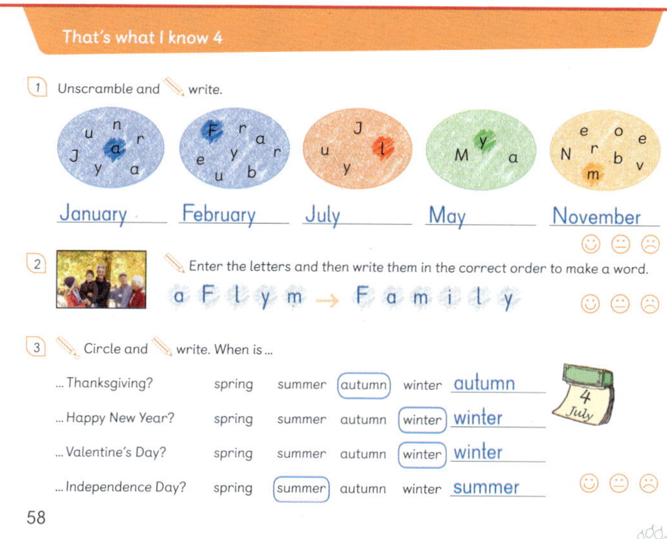

That's what I know 4

1 Unscramble and write.

u n r J a y a → January
F r a e y r u b → February
J u l y → July
y M a → May
e o e N r b v m → November

2 Enter the letters and then write them in the correct order to make a word.

a F l y m → F a m i l y

3 Circle and write. When is …

… Thanksgiving?	spring	summer	(autumn)	winter	autumn
… Happy New Year?	spring	summer	autumn	(winter)	winter
… Valentine's Day?	spring	summer	autumn	(winter)	winter
… Independence Day?	spring	(summer)	autumn	winter	summer

58

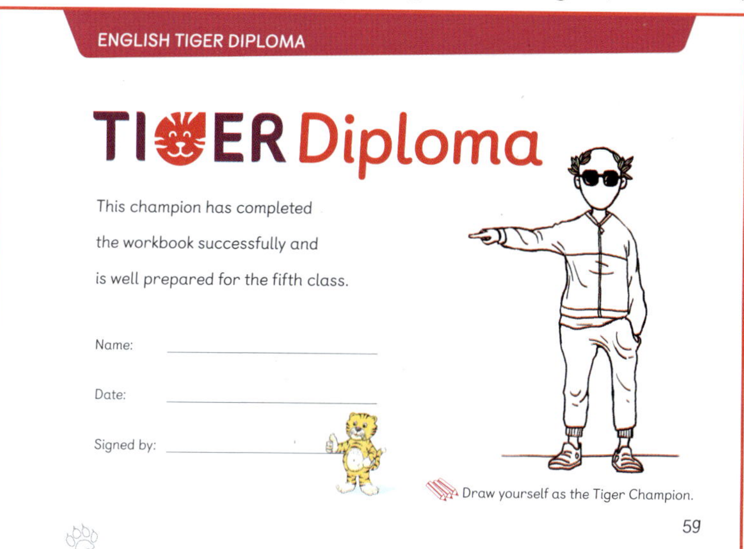

ENGLISH TIGER DIPLOMA

TIGER Diploma

This champion has completed the workbook successfully and is well prepared for the fifth class.

Name:

Date:

Signed by:

Draw yourself as the Tiger Champion.

59

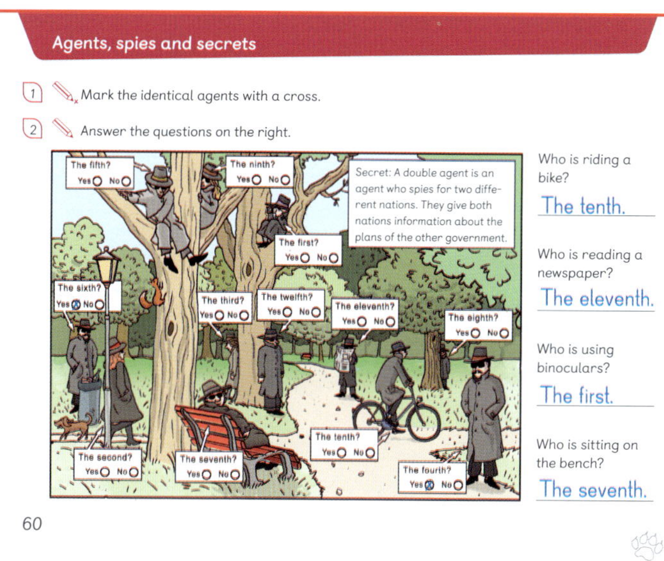

Agents, spies and secrets

1 Mark the identical agents with a cross.

2 Answer the questions on the right.

Who is riding a bike? The tenth.

Who is reading a newspaper? The eleventh.

Who is using binoculars? The first.

Who is sitting on the bench? The seventh.

60

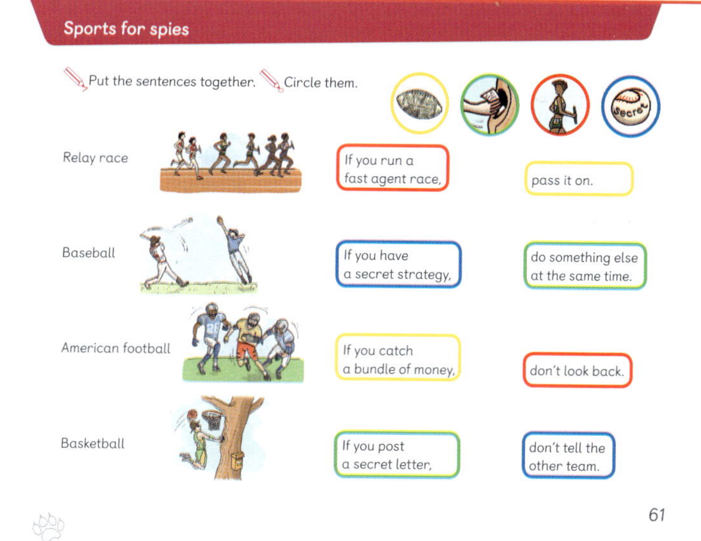

Sports for spies

Put the sentences together. Circle them.

Relay race	If you run a fast agent race,	pass it on.
Baseball	If you have a secret strategy,	do something else at the same time.
American football	If you catch a bundle of money,	don't look back.
Basketball	If you post a secret letter,	don't tell the other team.

61

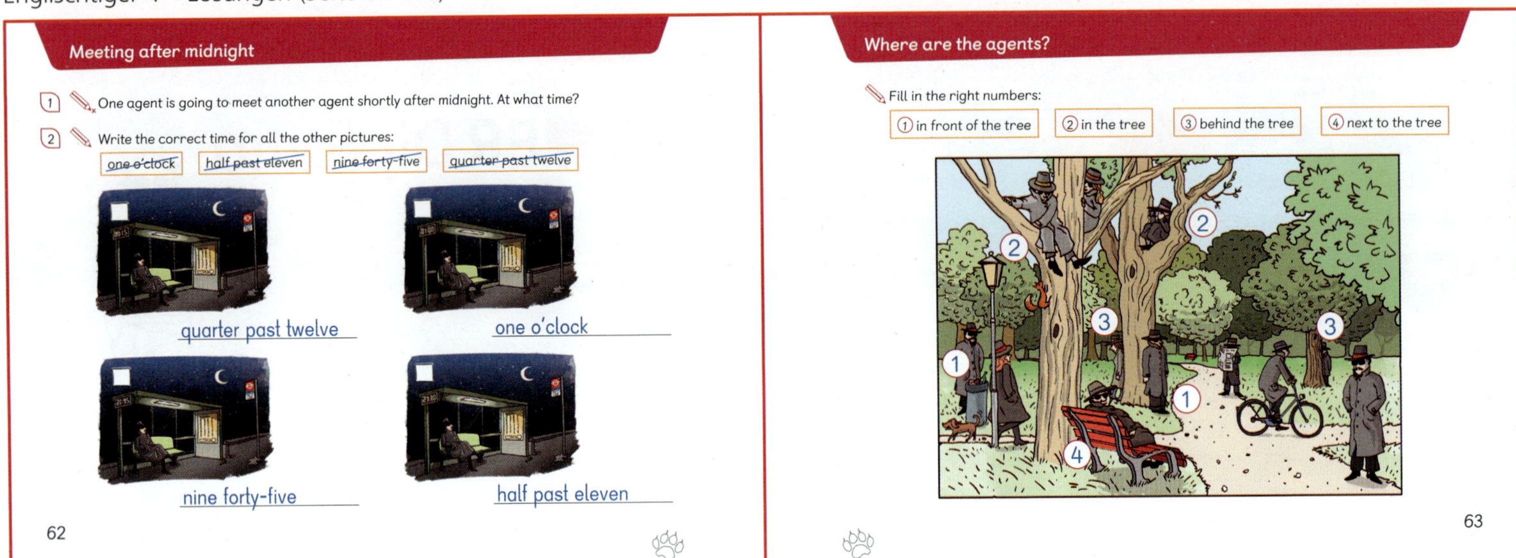
Meeting after midnight
1 One agent is going to meet another agent shortly after midnight. At what time?
2 Write the correct time for all the other pictures:
one o'clock
half past eleven
nine forty-five
quarter past twelve
quarter past twelve
one o'clock
nine forty-five
half past eleven
62
Where are the agents?
Fill in the right numbers:
1 in front of the tree
2 in the tree
3 behind the tree
4 next to the tree
63

Circle the animal tracks as the animals in the same colour.

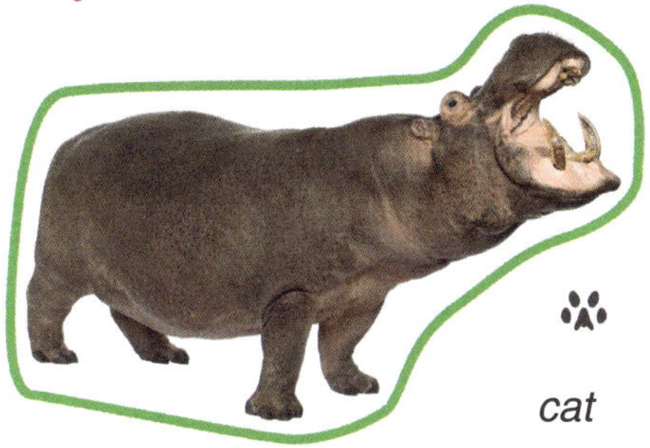

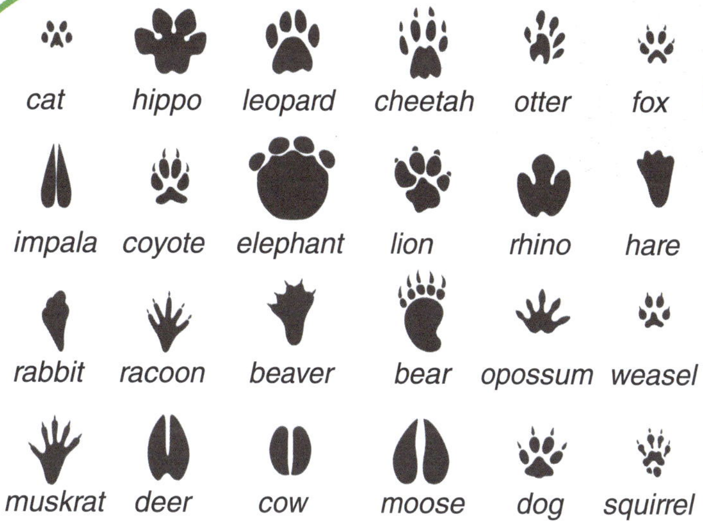

cat	hippo	leopard	cheetah	otter	fox
impala	coyote	elephant	lion	rhino	hare
rabbit	racoon	beaver	bear	opossum	weasel
muskrat	deer	cow	moose	dog	squirrel

Write the words that match the pictures:

alligator	beaver	horse	lizard	scorpion	squirrel

Whose tails are these?

This is a pony tail.

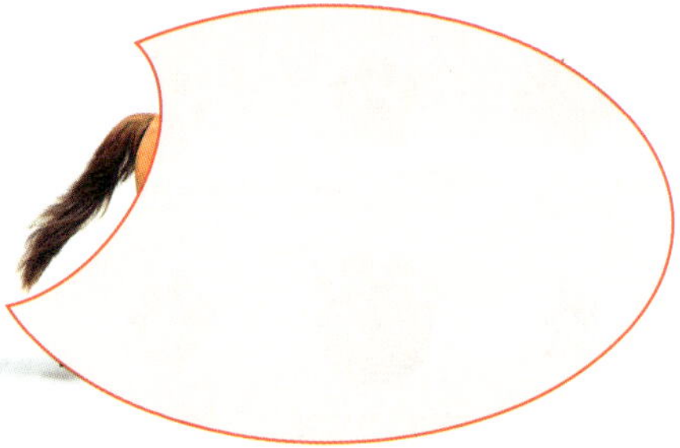

______________ tail

______________ tail

______________ tail

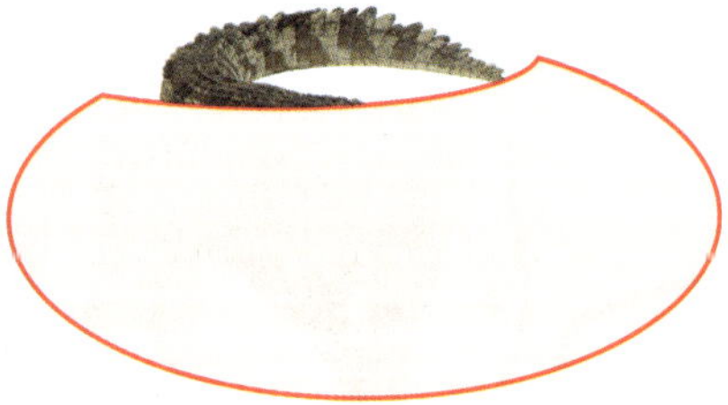

______________ tail

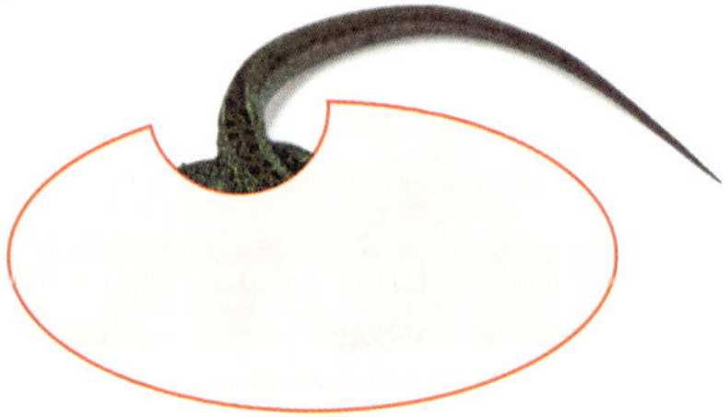

______________ tail

______________ tail

1 Circle the right word.

pitbull	jaguar	crocodile	shark
wild boar	deer	beaver	bear
piranha	hippo	tarantula	lion
lizard	lemur	crocodile	shark
tick	spider	frog	rat
lemur	wolf	macaque	owl
squirrel	shark	scorpion	beetle

2 How many legs do the circled animals have?

 ☐ two	☐ four	☐ six	☐ eight
 ☐ zero	☐ two	☐ four	☐ six
 ☐ zero	☐ two	☐ four	☐ six
 ☐ two	☐ four	☐ six	☐ eight
 ☐ zero	☐ two	☐ four	☐ six
 ☐ zero	☐ two	☐ four	☐ six
 ☐ four	☐ six	☐ eight	☐ ten

Connect the people who are talking to one another on the telephone.

Use symbols: ✚ ● ♥ ★

I love you, too!

Can I borrow your car?

I'm fine, thank you!

Ten o'clock tomorrow morning.

I love you!

How are you this morning?

Of course you can.

When is the next flight to LA?

Why ..., because ...

 Write:

She is ..., because ...

... is she angry?

... is he nervous?

... is he amazed?

... because her friend is having a baby.

She is happy, because her friend is having a baby.

... because he has won a trip to the USA.

... his wife is having a baby.

... because she has so much homework to do.

That looks really good.

envious ______ happy ______

~~happy~~ ~~envious~~

Write:

envious | tired | angry | nervous | happy

______

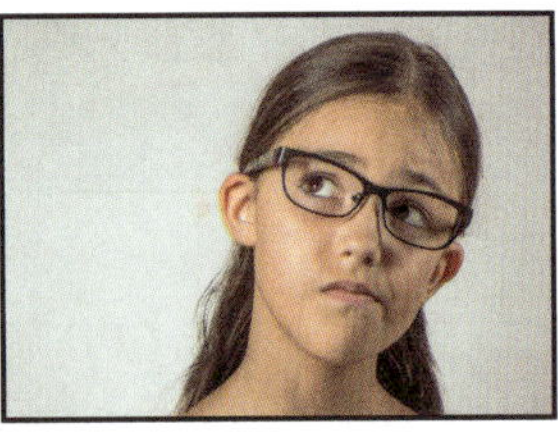

______

______

______

______

More feelings

 Write under the photos and  draw emoticons next to the pictures.

amazed | curious | happy | unsure | unhappy | quiet | cool

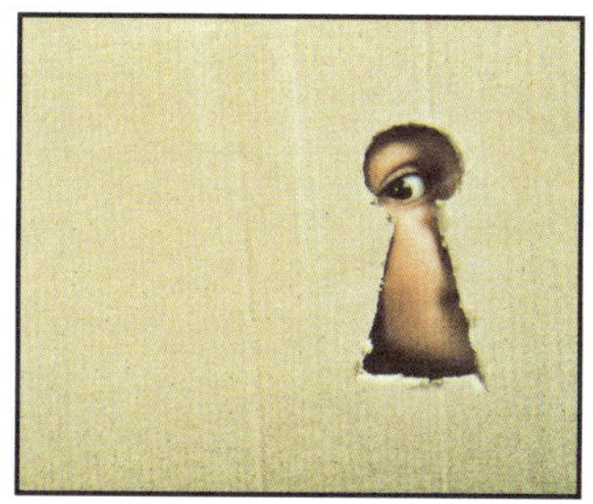
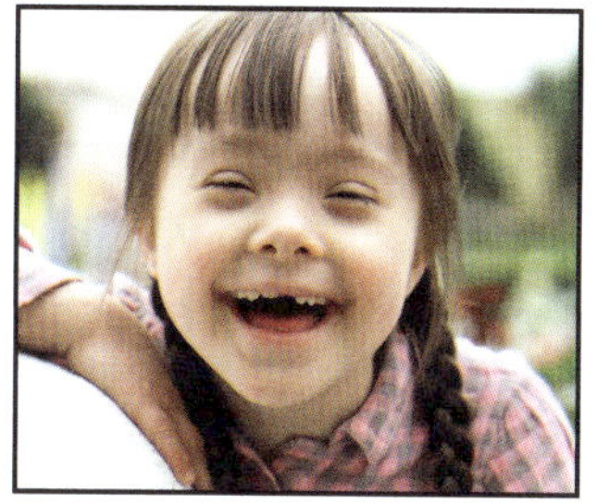

Interview with a friend

1 Draw a friend in your class.

Write on the lines.

Name: ____________________

Age: ______

2 Now ask the questions and write down the answers.

Yes, I do.

No, I don't.

Do you like walking in the dark? ____________ ____________

Do you like learning at school? ____________ ____________

Do you like climbing walls? ____________ ____________

Do you like watching football matches? ____________ ____________

Do you like horse riding? ____________ ____________

Do you like skateboarding? ____________ ____________

1 Circle the words match to the photos.

S	A	D	Y	T	I	R	E	D
M	Q	D	C	B	T	D	L	G
H	I	H	I	H	I	C	O	C
A	M	A	Z	E	D	Y	X	U
N	N	P	U	V	C	D	K	Z
G	O	P	T	W	B	E	J	I
R	P	Y	S	X	A	F	I	B
Y	Q	U	R	Y	Z	G	H	U
V	U	N	E	R	V	O	U	S

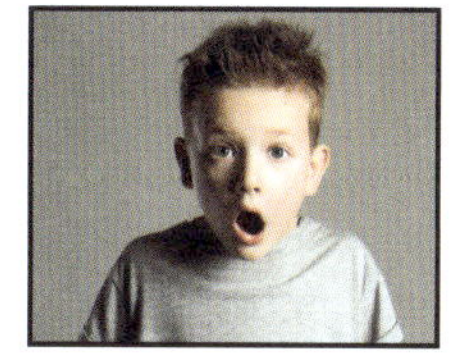

2 Find the words.

walking/climbingridingskateboardinglearningtelephoning

Write a shopping list for a delicious meal.
Choose chilli con carne or spaghetti bolognese:

spaghetti rice beans onions tomatoes garlic oregano
sweet pepper pepper salt minced meat ketchup

At the sports shop

Fill in the numbers and answer the questions.

① racket ② basketball ③ bike ④ riding helmet ⑤ inliner ⑥ basket ⑦ football ⑧ waveboard ⑨ hula hoop mature

What sport would you like to do? ______________________

What would you like to buy at the sports shop? ______________________

Are you a fan of a certain sport star? ______________________

What can you buy at a media store? ✎ Yes, I can buy … ☒ No, I won't get … ☐

tablets	☐ Yes	☐ No
notebooks	☐ Yes	☐ No
notepads	☐ Yes	☐ No
video games	☐ Yes	☐ No
board games	☐ Yes	☐ No
computers	☐ Yes	☐ No
comics	☐ Yes	☐ No
CDs and DVDs	☐ Yes	☐ No
cats and dogs	☐ Yes	☐ No
game consoles	☐ Yes	☐ No
game shows	☐ Yes	☐ No

What would you like to buy? ______________________________

At the convenience store

Mr. Sedda has a shop in Sydney, an Australian town.
He is very friendly and he has really a big range of goods.

1 Complete the conversation and answer the questions:

sixty   chewing gum   orange   day

Mr. Sedda | **You**

1 Good morning. Can I help you?

2 Good morning. Yes, I would like some ______________, please.

3 Orange or peppermint?

4 ______________

5 That will be ______________ cents. Thank you! Have a nice ________. Goodbye.

6 You too, Mr. Sedda. Goodbye.

2 Read the dialogue with a partner. Change roles.

1 Circle the words which don't belong to the other words.

- At the food store – let's cook:

CHAL: spaghetti CHOL: minced meat CHEL: tomatoes CHIL: comics

- At the sports shop – let's move on:

LO: bike LA: basket LI: ham and eggs LU: helmet

- At the electronics store – let's have fun:

CAN: tablets CUN: computers CIN: CDs and DVDs CON: rackets

- At the convenience store – let's chew something:

COR: chocolate CAR: cats and dogs CER: crisps CIR: chewing gum

- At the bakery – let's get something to eat:

NO: scones NA: bread NI: cake NE: money

The circled capital letters make a solution word.

____

1 Read and enter the right numbers.

◯ Hawaii became the 50th state in 1959. The Hawaiian flag contains the Union Jack.

◯ Texas has a simple flag containing the "Lone Star".

◯ Puerto Rico wants to join the USA. It would be the 51th state.

  Colour the flag.

The Star-Spangled Banner is the national flag of the United States of America.
The seven red and six white stripes symbolize the thirteen founding nations of the USA.
A new star was added for every new state.
The colours red, white and blue originate from the colours of the Union Jack.

New York landmarks

1 Fill in the right numbers.

(1) Statue of Liberty (2) Brooklyn Bridge (3) Empire State Building (4) Central Park

(5) Museum Of Modern Art (MOMA) (6) Times Square

  Which one would you like to visit? ______________________________

1 Find and write the right words.

hamburger|coleslawFrench fries
spare ribscolamilkshake

2 What do you like? Draw.

3 What do you like? Mark with a ☒ cross.

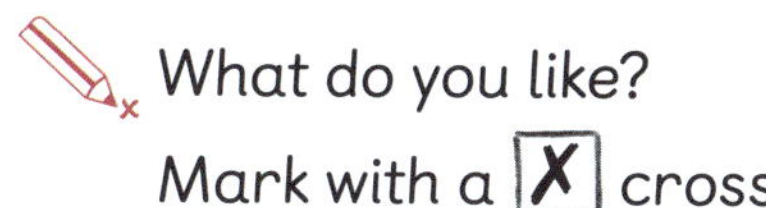

Read. Enter the right numbers.

1	backboard	vertical board with a basket attached
2	basket	the basket is a steel rim with a net attached to it
3	court	in international games 28 meters long and 15 meters wide
4	basketball	equipment
5	jersey	sport clothes
6	high-tops	shoes

Guy on the left: Dirk Nowitzki is a German basketball player for the Dallas Mavericks in the National Basketball Association (NBA). He is the highest-scoring non-American player in NBA history and the sixth player to achieve over 30,000 regular season points.

Guy on the right: Dennis Schroeder is a German basketball player for the Atlanta Hawks in the NBA. He formerly played for SG Braunschweig and Phantoms Braunschweig. He is widely regarded as one of the best talents in German basketball.

A popular American President

Enter the numbers and sing the anthem.

1. Barack Obama was the first black US President.
2. He is married to Michelle Obama.
3. They have two children: Malia Ann and Natasha.
4. The President of the United States lives in the White House in Washington, D. C.

American currency

1 How much is it?

_________ $

_________ ¢

1 half dollar ($)

1 quarter dollar ($)

1 cent ($)

1 dime ($)

5 cents ($)

1 dollar ($)

2 dollars ($)

5 dollars ($)

10 dollars ($)

50 dollars ($)

20 dollars ($)

2 How much money do you need?

	 A junior ticket: $ 26.50	 A visit: $ 14.00	 A portion: $ 3.00
 half dollar			
 1 dollar			
 2 dollars			
 5 dollars			
 10 dollars			

Tiger training 4

1 Colour the months and special days.

Merry Xmas	spring	January
Happy New Year	July	winter
Easter	October	
autumn	April	summer
Happy Halloween		

JanuaryFebruaryMarchAprilMayJuneJulyAugustSeptemberOctoberNovemberDecember

Happy VALENTINE'S Day!

Mother's Day

2 Find the months in the circle.

Which is your birthday month?

____

Thanksgiving Day

Read the text below. Match the words ● with the pictures ● and write the words.

Thanksgiving Day in the USA is celebrated on the 4th Thursday in November. It is an official holiday. Families come together and have a big feast with traditional food like roasted turkey, mashed potatoes or pumpkin pie. It goes back to the year 1615, when 38 English Pilgrim Fathers arrived with a ship in Virginia and celebrated their arrival with the Indians. The "Mayflower" was a famous ship of the Pilgrims, which arrived at Cape Cod on 21th November, 1620.

turkey	Mayflower	Pilgrim Fathers	family
●	●	●	●
●	●	●	●
______________	______________	______________	______________
______________	______________	______________	______________

Happy New Year

New Year's Day, also called simply New Year's, is observed on 1st January. It marks the start of a new year according to the Gregorian calendar. The start of New Year's Day is heralded by fireworks on the stroke of midnight, with parties and events, which are often televised.

1 Write the New Year's words:

Januaryfireworkspartiestelevisionmidnightfamilyfriendsholidays

January, ______________________________

____

2 How do you celebrate New Year's? ______________________________

____

Do you like fireworks? ☐ Yes ☐ No

1 Fill in the correct words.

FEBRUARY	LOVE	PRESENT	FLOWERS	HEART	CARD	CANDIES

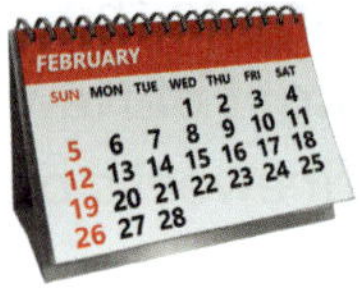

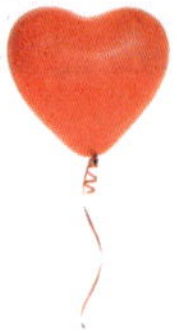

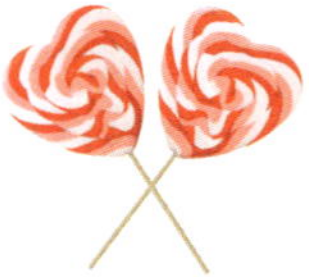

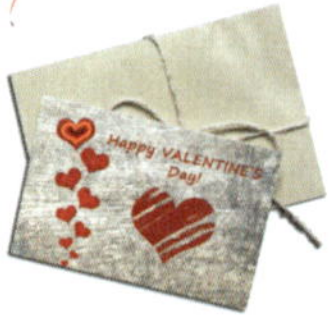

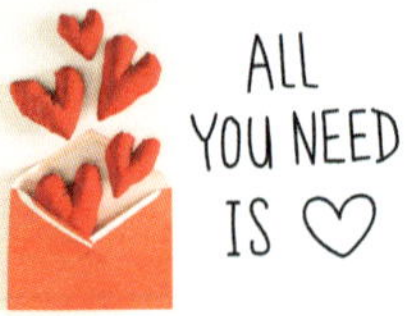

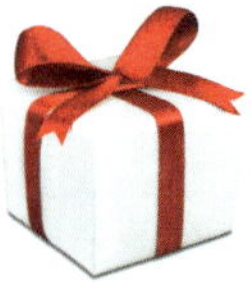

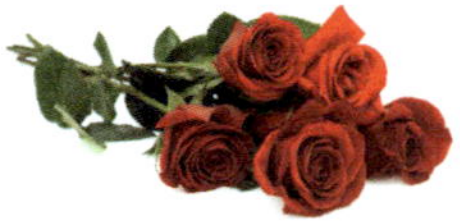

2 Which flowers can be a present for Valentine's Day? The grey letters make the solution.

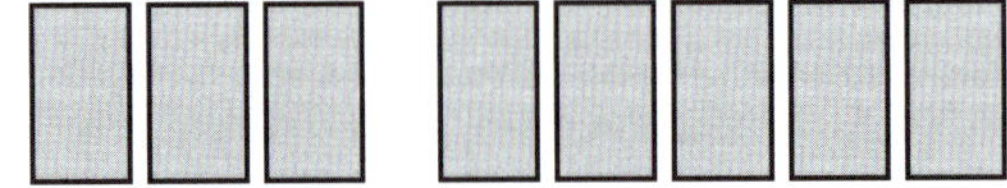

Read the text below. Match the words with the pictures and write the words.

The federal holiday of the United States celebrates the adoption of the Declaration of Independence on 4th July, 1776, which declared independence from the British Empire.

Stars and Stripes

Stars and Stripes | parades | feast | barbecues | fireworks | cake

1 Unscramble and write.

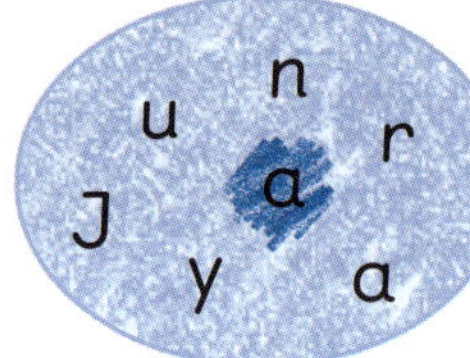

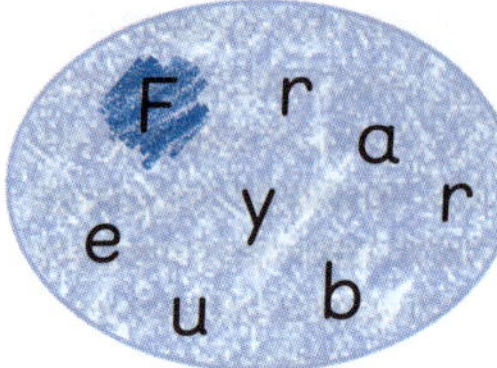

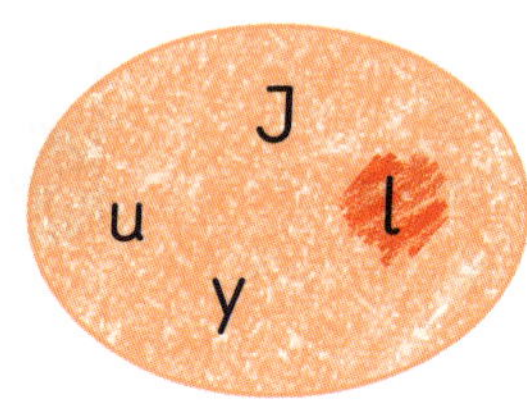

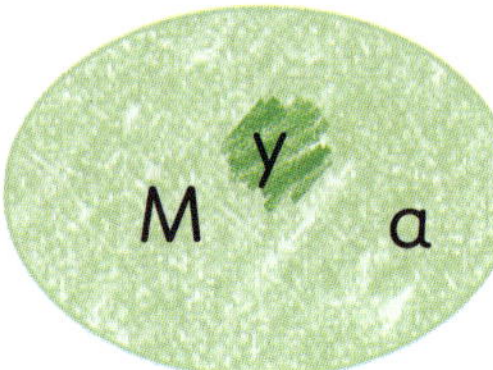

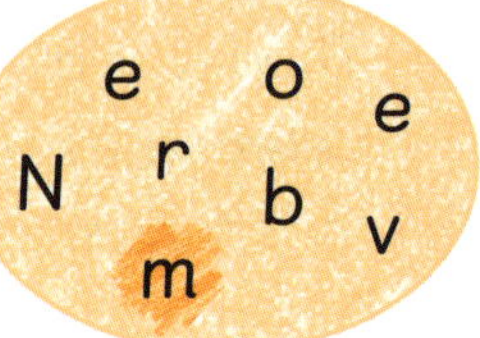

_______ _______ _______ _______ _______

2 

Enter the letters and then write them in the correct order to make a word.

3  Circle and  write. When is ...

... Thanksgiving?	spring	summer	autumn	winter	_______
... Happy New Year?	spring	summer	autumn	winter	_______
... Valentine's Day?	spring	summer	autumn	winter	_______
... Independence Day?	spring	summer	autumn	winter	_______

TIGER Diploma

This champion has completed

the workbook successfully and

is well prepared for the fifth class.

Name: ______________________

Date: ______________________

Signed by: ______________________

 Draw yourself as the Tiger Champion.

Agents, spies and secrets

1 Mark the identical agents with a cross.

2 Answer the questions on the right.

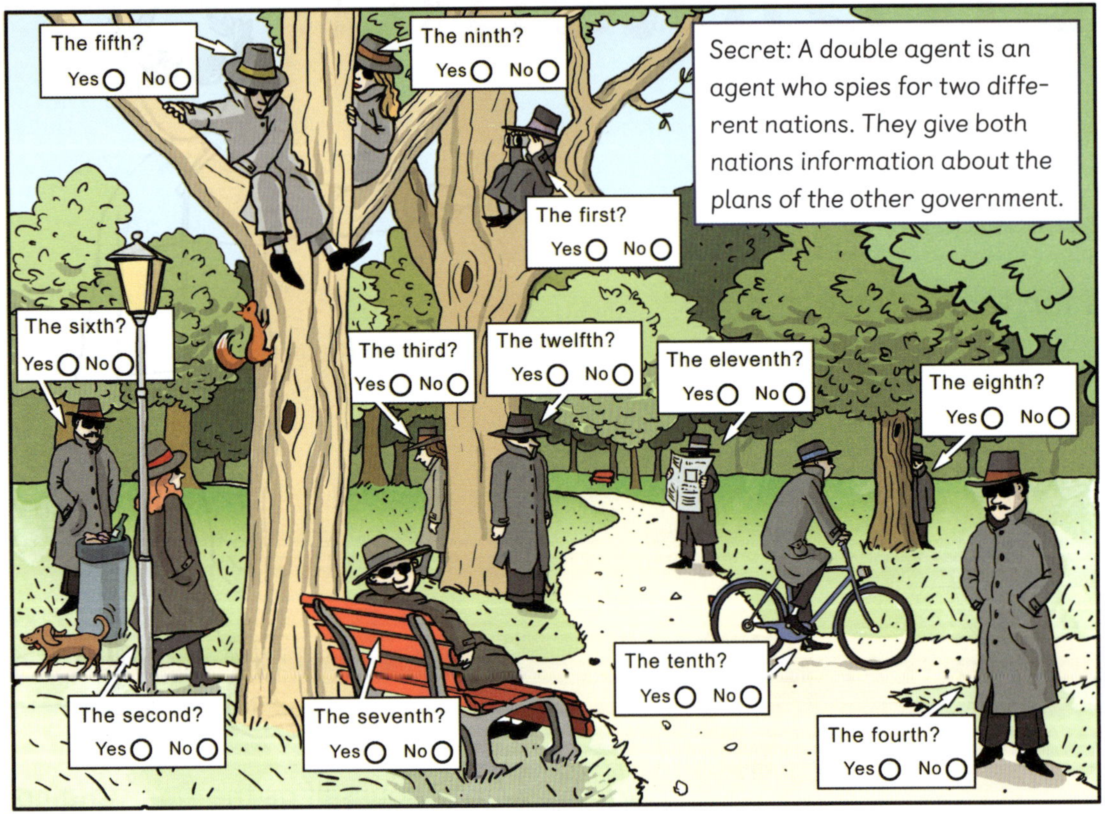

The fifth? Yes ◯ No ◯

The ninth? Yes ◯ No ◯

Secret: A double agent is an agent who spies for two different nations. They give both nations information about the plans of the other government.

The first? Yes ◯ No ◯

The sixth? Yes ◯ No ◯

The third? Yes ◯ No ◯

The twelfth? Yes ◯ No ◯

The eleventh? Yes ◯ No ◯

The eighth? Yes ◯ No ◯

The tenth? Yes ◯ No ◯

The second? Yes ◯ No ◯

The seventh? Yes ◯ No ◯

The fourth? Yes ◯ No ◯

Who is riding a bike?

____

Who is reading a newspaper?

____

Who is using binoculars?

____

Who is sitting on the bench?

____

 Put the sentences together.  Circle them.

Relay race  If you run a fast agent race, pass it on.

Baseball  If you have a secret strategy, do something else at the same time.

American football  If you catch a bundle of money, don't look back.

Basketball  If you post a secret letter, don't tell the other team.

Meeting after midnight

1 One agent is going to meet another agent shortly after midnight. At what time?

2 Write the correct time for all the other pictures:

one o'clock | half past eleven | nine forty-five | quarter past twelve

____

____

____

____

Where are the agents?

 Fill in the right numbers:

① in front of the tree	② in the tree	③ behind the tree	④ next to the tree

TIGER CODE

Auf den beiden Scheiben und bei den Englischtigern kannst du die Seiten abhaken, die du schon bearbeitet hast. Außerdem kannst du mit den Scheiben geheime Nachrichten schreiben: Kopiere sie und schneide sie aus. Dann stich mit einer Musterklammer in die Mitte der Scheiben ein Loch. Nun kannst du die beiden Scheiben aufeinanderlegen und mit der Musterklammer verbinden.
Biege die beiden Laschen nach außen, sodass die Scheiben fixiert sind. Wenn du nun die innere Scheibe drehst, kannst du aus dem Text der äußeren Scheibe einen verschlüsselten Text machen – z. B. aus „gut gemacht“ wird „KYX KIQEGLX“.

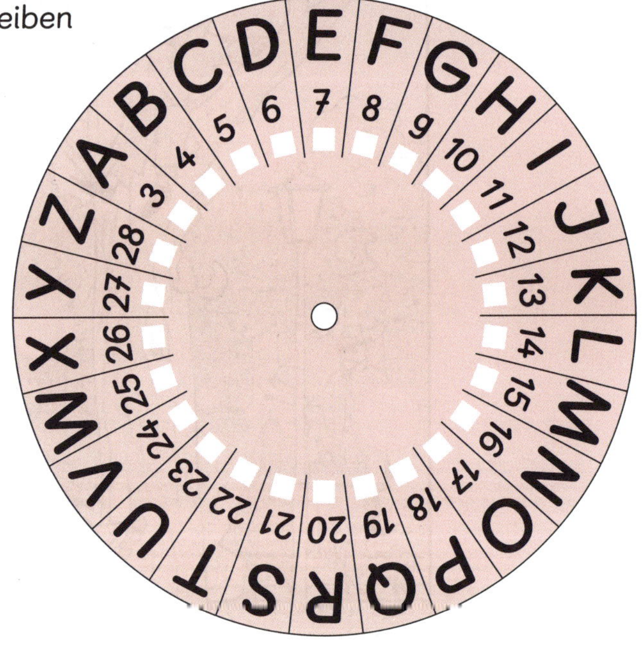